A
History
of
Deerpark
in
Orange County
New York

Peter E. Gumaer

HERITAGE BOOKS
2006

HERITAGE BOOKS
AN IMPRINT OF HERITAGE BOOKS, INC.

Books, CDs, and more—Worldwide

For our listing of thousands of titles see our website
at
www.HeritageBooks.com

A Facsimile Reprint
Published 2006 by
HERITAGE BOOKS, INC.
Publishing Division
65 East Main Street
Westminster, Maryland 21157-5026

Originally published by
The Minisink Valley Historical Society
1890

Index copyright © 1994 by Dan Burrows

— Publisher's Notice —
In reprints such as this, it is often not possible to remove blemishes from the original. We feel the contents of this book warrant its reissue despite these blemishes and hope you will agree and read it with pleasure.

International Standard Book Number: 978-0-7884-0082-7

Photo Credit: Richard G. Tarbell

Ethel K. Hornbeck

This reprinting of The History of Deerpark is dedicated to Ethel K. Hornbeck, treasurer of the Minisink Valley Historical Society for more than 20 years and a loyal and faithful member.

Preface

This reprinting brings back into public domain one of the earliest histories written in Orange County, New York. Written by Peter E. Gumaer between 1858 and 1862, the book was originally published by the Minisink Valley Historical Society in 1890 after Gumaer's son, Peter L. Gumaer, donated the manuscript to the Society. The society, formed in 1889, would regularly publish historical articles and booklets relating to the area's history during the first two decades of its existence. The reprinting of this book continues this long tradition of preserving our region's history.

The History of Deerpark remains a classic work and an important research tool not only for genealogists but also for those contemplating the lifestyles of Dutch settlers in the late 1690s and early 1700s. Gumaer's detailed account provides interesting reading, fascinating insights and offers the best historical perspective possible given that he knew people who were only a generation or two beyond the original settlement of the upper and lower neighborhoods. In addition, he provides a wealth of information about the region's geography and the lifestyles of Native Americans. His analysis of vital statistics is another important feature of the book.

This book has been reprinted once, by T. Emmet Henderson of Middletown, New York, in 1970, and the index for this edition has been prepared by Orange County Genealogical Society member Daniel H. Burrows who created it in 1994.

Peter Osborne
Executive Director
Minisink Valley Historical Society
September 1994

PREFACE.

Having been solicited by certain individuals of the first settlers in the neighborhood of my residence, in the town of Deerpark, for a written information in relation to their respective ancestry, both of those who now reside in this town and of those residing in other parts of our country, and feeling desirous to gratify their wishes and save from oblivion the knowledge I possess relative to their forefathers, I have thought proper to make out a small work of the same and get it printed, so that all who shall be desirous of such information can obtain the same, which undoubtedly must be a great satisfaction to many who have not had the opportunity of becoming informed in relation thereto, especially the descendants of those whose parents at an early day of the settlement of our western country emigrated into it. The general topics of conversation have changed much in this vicinity within my time of life. At the termination of the Revolutionary war this change commenced. The attention of the young people was generally directed towards the passing scenes of their time, and they remained ignorant of what had transpired during the lives of their forefathers. In the early part of my life some of the old people, whenever they came together, generally introduced the occurrences of former times, in relation to the ancient inhabitants of this valley, who inhabited it for a distance of eighty miles. From these discourses and my own observations and researches, I have become enabled to write this history. Capt. Cuddeback, Esq. Depuy and my own mother were the greatest historians. Of what had materially transpired throughout this valley from the first and last of these I have had my greatest source of information.

GUMAER'S OLD STONE HOUSE.

INTRODUCTION.

The most interesting subjects in relation to the town of Deerpark are contained in Eager's "History of Orange County." These are not embraced in this work, excepting a few articles for making a connection of certain matters therein contained, with additional materials herein introduced.

All mankind generally are desirous to possess a knowledge of their ancestry, their characters, occupations, manner and circumstances of life, the lineal descent of the most anterior of them, the different scenes through which the successive generations have passed, &c. All of which is embraced in this small work, as far as my information and knowledge in relation thereto extends; and, being an old man, and having in early life had great opportunities to become informed in respect to the early settlement of this town and of the people, who, from time to time settled in it, and their descendants from generation to generation, down to the parentage of the fourth of those who first settled in Peenpack, and of the third who settled in the lower neighborhood. I, myself, have also been a spectator of the transpiring occurrences from the commencement of the Revolutionary war until the present time.

Very different have been the scenes of life through which the successive generations have passed, and, considering myself to possess the greatest fund of knowledge relating to the same, I have viewed it as incumbent on me to write this history and save from oblivion the matter therein contained, in such manner as the incompetency of my abilities will admit, which, even if not in the best manner, still comprehend the substance I deemed necessary to be embodied in it, with much diffidence, however, in respect to some parts of the same, in which I have been too lavish in introducing unnecessary matter. But as this work is only intended for the present and future descendants of the first pioneers in the district of the present town of Deerpark, I have thought proper to enter some minute matters to inform the readers how their forefathers have progressed through life. They came here poor and ventured their lives among the Indians to enjoy the lands they took in possession and afterwards bought.

The materials furnished in this work are the following : My views relative to an alteration supposed to have, in very remote times, occurred in this valley and created the formation of it, so as our forefathers found it; also the time they settled here and the inhabitants who then occupied it ; their manner of life and means of supporting themselves, and other different matters and conjectures in relation to them ; also the wild animals, fowls and fishes which were in this part of the country; the names of the first seven settlers, and the time they procured a patent for the land they intended to occupy; also the names of those who first settled in the lower neighborhood, and, as near as can be ascertained, the time they settled there and the places where all of both neighborhoods severally located; also the names of their respective descendants to the third generation of the Peenpack neighborhood, their marriages and manner of living, and the ages to which they respectively arrived, as near as I could ascertain the same. Also certain matters in relation to a late emigration into this town of inhabitants who have built up the village of Port Jervis, which commenced about the year 1827; the great diminution of birds, snakes. frogs and toads, within the last thirty years; also the commencement and continuance from time to time of religious worship, and the first introduction of Justices of the Peace, &c.; the anterior prices of farmers' productions, and of wages, together with some speculative and interesting matters in relation to the same.

NOTE.—There were some members of families in both neighborhoods whose names I did not know, and have left blanks for the same, so that the purchaser of a book can write the names of his respective relatives, omitted in the blanks left for that purpose.

[The committee on publication have supplied these names, so far as they have been able, and have included them in brackets in their proper places.]

The "History of Deerpark" was written by Mr. Gumaer between the years of 1858 and 1862 from materials collected by him during many years of close observation and after much diligence and painstaking in the collection of facts derived from frequent intercourse with others. It is safe to say that no other person in the town of Deerpark, within the last fifteen years, has been so well qualified by the possession of historical facts and other considerations to write its history as was Mr. Gumaer. Samuel W Eager, in his history of Orange county, published in 1846 and 1847, says that he is more indebted to Mr. Gumaer than to any one person in the county for his " good will and assistance " in preparing his history. This work, prepared with so much care, has been very generously donated by his son, Peter L. Gumaer, to the Minisink Valley Historical Society, who have deemed it of sufficient value to publish, and appointed a committee to superintend its publication. This committee have found it necessary to make a few changes in the correction of dates, which have been found to be erroneous, as also in a few instances in the names of persons and of places occupied by them. Where blanks have been left by the author in the names of families, to which he alludes in his introduction, the committee have endeavored to fill them, so far as they have been able, from church records and other sources. Where any blanks remain unfilled, or where there may be any errors in the filling up, or in the original, the committee will esteem it a favor to be informed of the same. The changes that have been thus made are indicated either by the names being inclosed in brackets or by explanatory notes at the bottom of the page. As the history was written about thirty years ago, Mr. Gumaer designates particular places by their then owners and occupants. As these have, in many instances, undergone changes by death and removal, the committee have added notes indicating the present owners and occupants. With these exceptions and an occasional word or two, the history is published as originally written.

The committee close this statement with a brief sketch of the author :

Peter E. Gumaer was born in the town of Deerpark, at or near Fort Gumaer, May 28, 1771, and died December 18, 1869, at the age of 98 years, 6 months and 20 days. His parents were Ezekiel Gumaer and Naomi Low. He was a descendant of the French Huguenots, who fled from France at the time of their persecution. His father, being a farmer, he inherited the business and also learned the art of surveying, which he followed for more than fifty years. He surveyed most of the lands in the town of Deerpark, and also of adjoining towns. He was plain and unassuming in manner and deportment, much attached to his home and family, and, during his whole lifetime, lived in the town of Deerpark, having never visited the city of New York. In his principles he was regarded as a man of great integrity, always manifesting a conscientious regard for right, and nothing but strict and exact justice would satisfy him. His habits of living were extremely temperate, using but little animal food and no stimulants, except tea. He was a man of great industry, never idle and never seeking pleasure or enjoyment outside of business or study. He was of a literary turn of mind, and devoted as much of his time to reading and study as his pursuits would allow. He took great delight in the study of astronomy and philosophy. He was especially interested in Sir Isaac Newton's theory of the motions of the heavenly bodies, and said if it was correct, perpetual motion was possible and sought for a long time to demonstrate it practically. In 1851 he published a small volume upon astronomy. During his life he held many positions of public trust, which were filled with credit to himself and to the satisfaction of his constituents. It is said that among the many instruments of writing drawn by him not one was ever broken in a court of law, nor were any of his surveys of land found to be incorrect.

He held in high esteem his ancestry, whose remains are buried in the Gumaer Cemetery, and a few years previous to his death, as a token of regard for them, he erected monuments to their memory with appropriate inscriptions.

In his early life it was customary for the ministers in the Reformed Dutch Church, which he attended, to preach in the Holland (Dutch) and English languages on alternate Sabbaths, and so familiar was he with the former that upon returning home he was at a loss to say, when asked, in which language the services had been held. A bit of romance has been related concerning his marriage. It is said that when he was a young man he visited the house of his future mother-in-law, and that she had a little child in the cradle which she was rocking, and that she said to him: "Peter, I want you to rock the cradle, and when this child grows up to be a young woman you may have her for a wife." It so proved that he married this same child that he had thus rocked in the cradle.

The names and ages of Mr. Gumaer's children are as follows :

Morgan, born January 27th, 1815, and died July 5th, 1855.

Ezekiel P., born May 10th, 1817, and died June 25th. 1877.

Jacob.C. E., born October 18th, 1820, living at Ovid, Mich.

Peter L., born January 29th, 1827, living at Guymard, N. Y.

Naomi, born January 20th, 1830, and died May 2d, 1862.

Andrew J., born November 4th, 1833, living at Guymard, N. Y.

Esther Harriet, born August 30th, 1835, living at Brooklyn, N. Y., widow of Isaac Mulock.

HISTORY OF DEERPARK.

GEOGRAPHICAL FORMATION OF THE VALLEY.

Before entering into a detail relative to the settlement of this town by Europeans, the causes of their emigration from the fatherland, their manner of life in this then wilderness part of our country, &c., &c., I will give my views of what I consider to have been anteriorly the geographical face of this district of territory, its productions and its native inhabitants.

The present form of the surface of the earth teaches us that there has been a time when it was in many places very different from what it is at this day. This appears to be the case wherever there are rivers and streams of water ; and we have reason to think that many lakes and ponds have been drained by the action of streams of water issuing therefrom. It must be the case that there was a time when the surface of the ground in the valley along the Neversink and Delaware rivers in this town, together with that part of it which extends southwest to the gap of the mountain, where the Delaware passes through it, and northeast to the North river, &c., laid below the bottom of a lake of water. This opinion has been formed previous to my contemplations respecting it. Eager gives some account of this in his "History of Orange County," pages 407 and 408, and sufficiently establishes the fact from Indian tradition, &c.

Not only does the gap of the mountain, where the river passes through it, exhibit strong reasons of a passage being worn through it by the action of the water of a lake in this valley, but the knolls and low hills in this valley show that they have undergone much washing of water; and, what appears somewhat mysterious, hills thirty and forty feet higher than the surface of the river flats are all composed of ground, gravel, sand and such smooth stones as are in the bottoms of rivers, from which it appears that not only the surface of those hills, but that all the materials of which they are composed. have for some length of time been water-washed. We find in them some places of clear sand, not mixed with the other materials mentioned, such as is in river sand banks; from which we have reason to conjecture that after the water received a passage through the mountain it created a current in the lake towards it, and as that passage enlarged and wore down, the water in the lake drew off and the current of its stream increased and washed the highest parts of its bottom down into the hollows, where the water was deep, and thereby run down gradually large bodies of water-washed stones, gravel, sand and ground from the highest elevations of the bottom surface into its lowest parts, many of which have remained where they have been carried by the waters, and the adjoining ground, which first was highest, has run down the stream and continued to be moved down until a gradual descent of the rivers was formed, on a bottom of smooth water-washed stones, gravel and sand, which now lie at different depths below the surface of the river flats, viz.: from about four to seven and eight feet below that of the lands along the Neversink river, and at greater depths along the surface of the Delaware river flats.

After a river bottom was formed where the flats now are, the stream creating meandering channels through those river bottom flats would contain the water of the rivers when low, but in freshets, overflow the flat bottoms, whereby in every freshet a part of the ground which the water carried down in such times, lodged on the surface of those flats, which, continuing to accumulate in this way for a great length of time, raised the surface so high that the freshets did not overflow it, unless partially in uncommon high water; and as the waters became more and more confined in stationary channels, the bottoms of these wore down by the action and weight of the water. In this manner undoubtedly was formed the soil of our river lands. In the vicinity of the gap of the Shawangunk mountain, through which the New York & Erie Railroad passes, are indications in some places on the east side of the mountain of the surface of the ground having in a very remote period of time been under water, when I contemplate it ran through this gap into the valley west of the mountain into a lake which has been mentioned.

All rivers and streams have formed the grade of their bottoms from their smmmits toward the ocean according to their magnitude, and the original formation of the respective districts of country through which they pass.

The river flats, amounting to about three or four thousand acres, was nearly all the land in this town which the first pioneers considered to be of any value for agricultural purposes, the residue being generally mountainous, rough, stony land, was by them considered to be of no value for farming purposes.

PLENTIFUL SUPPLY OF GAME, FISH, FRUIT, ETC.

This district of territory which the small town of Deerpark now embraces, when the Indians were its sole proprietors, was a very plentiful place for Indian life when first discovered by Europeans. The flats, covered with a tall grass from four to six feet high, and the same and surrounding woods, often burned over, abounded with numerous deer, bears, raccoons, and many smaller animals suitable for the sustenance of man, also with turkeys, ducks, partridges and other birds suitable for man's diet. Generally in the spring of the year vast numbers of pigeons passed over here to the northeast, vast flocks of which generally lighted on the trees and ground to get food, which gave opportunities of killing some of them. The rivers and brooks teemed with different kinds of fishes, such as trout, pike, chubs, suckers, sunfish, catfish and eels, and numerous shad in the spring season in both the Delaware and the Neversink rivers, in the latter of which they ran up about five miles, which distance then generally was deep water and extended to where David Swartwout now lives*; these fish were caught by bush seines, and in the Delaware river were also many rockfish, which were taken in the fall of the year by means of eel-weirs and bush seines, some of which were the largest fish in this part of that river. Also, there were, and still are, different kinds of nuts, such as white walnuts, hickory nuts, chestnuts, butternuts hazelnuts; also various kinds of fruit and berries, to wit: large and small grapes, plums, black and red wild cherries, huckleberries, strawberries, black and red raspberries, blackberries of two or more kinds, and wintergreen berries. Such was this district of country and its productions when our forefathers came here, so that they could obtain a plentiful supply of the best of wild meats of animals, fowls and fishes, and, by the cultivation of small portions of their lands, they could obtain a supply of grain, roots and other vegetables. They could not do much at farming before the children of these first families became able to assist in that business. At this early period of their settlement they pounded their grain for such bread, cakes and soups as they made in those times, for doing which they procured pounding stones from the Indians, who manufactured them, and made or obtained from the Indians pounding blocks from one and a half to two and a half feet long, and about ten inches in diameter, in one end of which a suitable round cavity was burned in which to pound their grain, coarse salt, &c. The Indians manufactured both the stones and blocks in good style.

---

* Now (1889) the residence of Peter D. Swartwout.

Jacob Cuddeback built a small mill on a spring brook near his residence. How it answered the purpose of grinding is not known. One of the stones in my possession (now broken) was about two feet in diameter and about two inches thick. It was found in a cellar of an old house which stood near Cuddeback's first residence.

The animals, fowls and fishes probably did not diminish whilst the Indians were the only inhabitants of this part of the country. The increase of these people was slow. A married couple generally did not have more than two or three children, in consequence of which they did not become more thickly populated than to consume only a small proportion of the abundance of wild meat this part of the country continued to produce, and they, not having the means we have to kill and get the wild animals, fowls and fishes, often suffered in consequence of not being enabled to kill as many as they wanted for their support. The most dexterous of them could generally get a plentiful supply, but those who were inactive had sometimes to be assisted by the others, especially in the cold season of the year.

INDIANS.

When we take a view of the difference between the acquirements of the Indian race of people and those of our own nation, and the European and other enlightened nations of the world, we behold an endless acquisition which the industry and perseverance of the latter have brought into their possession, whilst the former have scarcely made a remove from a state of infancy in respect to improvements. This we cannot so much ascribe to their mental abilities as to their indolence and distaste of the pursuits of our people, preferring their own mode of life to that of ours. They were in a state of great destitution before their intercourse with Europeans for want of such materials as they were enabled to procure after Europeans settled among them, from whom they could obtain such materials as were necessary for their livelihood, guns, traps, hatchets, knives, blankets, and other articles of which they stood in need, whereby their condition of life was much improved; and these advantages which they derived and which their descendants still continue to obtain as mentioned, were, and continue to be of greater benefit to these people than the territories which they abandoned; for they now have the means of obtaining a more comfortable living than what they had before Europeans came into this country. Yet we must admit that it was a disagreeable and melancholy trial for them to leave their native places; but for these sacrifices they have received and continue to receive a good reward, of which they would have remained destitute if they had remained alone in this country. It is the lot of mankind to undergo such changes. Thousands of foreigners and our own citizens are continually migrating from place to place to advance their interest and better their condition in life. Before Europeans came into this country, stone, wood and clay were the only materials of which they manufactured any implements for their use; and stone axes, bows and arrows were the most valuable articles they manufactured. The stone axe was made of a solid stone, about six inches long and two thick, one end round and the other flattened with a rounding towards its edge, which was made as sharp as the nature of the stone would bear for its intended use. With these they would get bark from trees to cover their wigwams, and made other shelters under which to evade the inclemency of storms of snow and rain, night air, &c.; also to get bark for canoes, and girdle trees to kill them, so that the bark and limbs would fall for fuel. And with these axes in a slow operation they could cut and split small saplings for bows, and with these and other sharp stones and bones could scrape them off to a required thickness. Arrow heads (generally called harpoons in this section) were made of different kinds of flint stones, from three to about four inches long, one inch wide at the large end, and tapering from that to the small end. They were flat and rounding towards each side for sharpening the edges; a notch was worked into each side of the big end to fasten it into the arrow. These appear to have been made by knocking off small scales, whereby their surfaces, were left uneven.

It was said that they had manufactured pots of clay for cooking, and that a few remains of these had been found, in a broken condition, and that they made eel-pots of withs and caught therein eels and fish by setting them in the mouths of eel-weirs, which consisted of wings of stones thrown up in rivers and streams of water. The stone axes, bows and arrows were of great value to the naked-handed Indians. With the latter it was said that they could even kill a deer by making the bow very stiff and laying down with it in the tall grass which grew on the flats near to a deer-path, would, when a deer approached to pass, place both feet against the bow and with both hands draw the string or cord of the bow and shoot the deer as it passed, so as to kill it. It was said they made use of a sharp flint stone to skin it.

Now, although the improvements the natives of this country had made during their existence in it was very trifling, yet they had attained to about all that was in their reach in the circumstances under which they labored, and had come to the borders of a gigantic step which was necessary to be made for entering into a field of improvements similar to that of the enlightened nations of the world.

MANUFACTURE OF IMPLEMENTS OF IRON AND STEEL.

This step is the manufacturing of iron from the ore, and iron and steel utensils. The most ingenious of our own race of people would be puzzled to get into operation any works to answer that purpose, naked-handed as those people were, and in their state of ignorance when alone in this country. This discovery of manufacturing iron and steel utensils is the most useful to mankind of any ever made. Without the manufacture of iron, or some other metal which would have answered the same purpose, mankind must all have remained in that low, naked-handed and unimproved state in which the Indians were found in this country. The production of this metal by the original cause of all things, and its manufacture, are indispensable for the whole business of mankind. The blacksmith and manufacturer of iron and steel stand at the head of all other mechanics. If the productions of the former were to pass out of existence, that of the latter would inevitably become extinct and the farmer would have to abandon the cultivation of the earth, and the wheels of all the hydraulic works and manufacturing machineries whatever would cease to move. The oceans, seas, lakes and rivers would become unburdened of the ships and vessels passing thereon; the rattling of cars on the railroads would stop their music, and the still voice of the telegraph would cease to whisper its news. The consequence of all of which would be starvation and a miserable life of such as should survive to witness such a terrible catastrophe.

From all of which we are taught the great blessing we have derived in being suitably formed for its manufacture, and the construction of innumerable articles for our use and advantage, new inventions of which are continually exhibited.

Dr. Franklin, a lover of science and friend of man, in the latter part of his life said, that after a century from the time of his decease he would like to revisit the earth to see what improvements would be made in that time. If he now, after a shorter period, should be reinstated on earth in his former capacity, he undoubtedly would be astonished at the vast mechanical improvements made in our country since his time, and his philanthrophy would receive the very pleasing satisfaction of having himself made a discovery from which has originated one of the most wonderful discoveries ever made, viz.: to convey intelligence instantaneously over any distance on our globe.

Now, although the Indians still remain disposed to

pursue their own habits of life, yet it appears obvious that the time will come when it will be necessary for their descendants to become an improved and educated people and to get a livelihood by agriculture, manufacture and literature ; for they, as well as ourselves, are susceptible of such improvements. Their habits of life, continued from generation to generation for a very great length of time, seem to have become so seated in their minds that all the entreaties which the white people have from time to time made to abandon their present mode of life and pursue that of ours, has had but little effect on the great body of Indians to lead them out of the long accustomed habits of their ancestry.

As they were scattered over all parts of this country before Europeans came into it, and, as their increase has been slow, it is evident that their origin in it must have been in a very remote period of time. They generally were most numerous where the animals, fowls and fishes on which they lived were most plentiful, which was in the vicinity of rivers and streams of water, lakes and ponds; and, in consequence of living chiefly on those natural productions and their destitution of the means to get a sufficient supply of these, made it necessary for them to scatter thinly over this part of our country for procuring a competency for their subsistence. It was said they raised corn and beans in very small quantities.

We have accounts of the South American Indians manufacturing vessels and trinkets of gold before Europeans came into it, in such parts of that country and its islands where that metal was plenty. This would have been easily done with the use of stones, as the same is very ductile.

FIRST SETTLERS.

In the year 1690, as near as can be determined, Jacob Cuddeback, Thomas Swartwout, Anthony Swartwout, Bernardus Swartwout, Peter Gumaer, John Tyse and David Jamison†, settled in the present town of Deerpark, in the County of Orange and State of New York, on and near a handsome knoll or hill contiguous to a spring brook and a spring of living water, in the central part of the Peenpack flats ‡. This spring still remains near its first location, but not as flush as formerly. The upper surface of this hill is flat, and its elevation about 20 feet higher than the lowland surrounding it. The Indian name, " Peenpack," was, by certain of the ancient people, said to be significant of this hill and spring.

Peter Gumaer located himself at the southwest end of the hill, John Tyse between that and the spring brook, Bernardus Swartwout on the easterly brow of the hill, a few rods westerly of the spring, where the cellar now remains; Thomas Swartwout on the central

---

† Tyse and Jamison, it appears from other sources of information, did not become permanent settlers here. Jamison was from Scotland, and, from 1697 to 1714, served either as Vestryman or Warden in Trinity Church, New York, where he was Recorder of the city in 1712, and Attorney-General of the Province of New York in 1720. Tyse (Tyson) lived at Kingston.

‡ About three-fourths of a mile south of the old stone house, which stands near A. E. Godeffroy's dwelling, all of which was formerly owned by Peter E. Gumaer and family. Fort Gumaer was located on the south end of this knoll, on which spot now stands the frame dwelling owned by A. J. Gumaer, of Guymard, and occupied by a tenant.

part of the hill, opposite the spring, where the cavity of his cellar remains ; Jacob Cuddeback a few rods northeast of the northeast end of the hill, on the low ground, where has been a cavity of his cellar, now leveled ; Anthony Swartwout, where the house formerly of Cornelius Van Inwegen stood, a few rods northeast of Cuddeback's place of residence, and David Jamison, somewhere near this last location. Here these few families had advantageously located themselves for material assistance to repel Indian attacks, in case they should happen, and also for all of them to get water out of the spring for their drink in hot weather. The most distant of those residences was not over thirty rods from it.

Eager, in making researches for a history of Orange County, found this settlement to be the earliest of any in it*. The liberty of settling here was probably obtained from the Indians by purchase ; for it appears that these settlers were and remained at peace with them and on friendly terms until the commencement of the French war. As the neighborhood in time extended about four miles in length, it continued to bear that name, although there were several localities within

---

* Since then it has been ascertained that there was an earlier settlement in the county near New Windsor, at what is known as Plum Point. In 1684, Patrick McGregorie, his brother-in-law David Toshuck, who subscribed his name " Laird of Minivard," and twenty-five others principally Sc tch Presbyterians, purchased a tract of 4,000 acres, embracing lands on both sides of Murderer's creek. Here, on Coùwanham's Hill, so-called from its aboriginal owner, but now known as Plum Point, McGregorie built his cabin, and in the same vicinity were those of his associates, William Chambers, William Sutherland and one Collum, while on the north side of the creek David Toshuck and his servant Daniel Maskrig established a trading post. (See Ruttenber's History of Orange County, p. 21, 22)

that distance which had other Indian names ; one at my present residence ; one at the Neversink river, near the aqueduct of the canal ; one at the present residence of Col. Peter P. Swartwout †, and two between that and the first Peenpack locality. In these several places resided small collections of Indians near living springs and streams of water.

When this place was first settled, it was about 25 or 30 miles distant from the nearest settlement of white people, which latter was on the road from here to Kingston. Two of the first pioneers, Cuddeback and Gumaer, were from France and of families who were in comfortable circumstances of life, which appears evident from what has been said by them in relation thereto, and from the fact that they had been brought up without doing any manual labor. It was said that their hands were so soft and tender when they first came into America that they blistered and bled when they first labored for a living in this country. The family of Cuddeback were in a trading business, in which Cuddeback had served as clerk. It was said the family of Gumaer were rich and in possession of large bills of exchange, for which they could not get money before he had to flee to escape persecution or death. From a certificate of his, in the French language, in relation to his church membership and character, dated the 20th of April, 1686, it appears that he then was in France and about 20 years of age. In 1685, the edict of Nantes was revoked by Louis XIV., King of France, whereby the Huguenots became unprotected by the laws of that country and exposed to the vengeance of

---

† Now (1889) owned and occupied by Benjamin Swartwout.

the Catholics, who were the most numerous and powerful class of people in that country, and, after they became unrestrained, exercised their power to torture and murder the former, and to plunder and destroy their property, which caused a flight of thousands of them from France into other countries, in which the two individuals mentioned made their escape from it.

The name Cuddeback, as now written and Codeback as written in the patent, must both differ from the original orthography. Cuddeback has said that his name was that of a certain city in France. On examining an ancient gazetteer I find the orthography of one city in that country to be "Caudebec," which, in the French tongue, has the same oral sound as that of Codeback in the English tongue.

The Rev. Henry Morris, of Cuddebackville, has furnished me with some historical accounts from Malte Brun's Universal Geography, Vol. 6, being the following notice of Caudebec :

"Caudebec was formerly the capitol of Caux, a small country in which agriculture has attained to a high degree of perfection, where every house, surrounded by trees of different sorts, contributes to adorn the different sites ; indeed, the country, watered by the Seine from Havre to Rouen, may vie with the vaunted banks of the Seine. Caudebec was a flourishing town before the revocation of the edict of Nantes ; it was almost ruined in consequence of that impolitic measure, and, although it possesses a convenient harbor, the population does not exceed three thousand souls. It is situated in the district of Yvetot, a small town of which the lords before the reign of Louis XI.

were styled kings by their vassals."

Morris further states that "Caudebec is situated in the department of the Lower Seine, in which are the following towns: Lillebonne, Rouen, Elbeuf, Gournay and Aumale," and judges that it lies on the river Seine between Paris and the English Channel, and belongs to that part of France that anciently was called Normandy.

I feel very thankful for this information. It reminds me of certain occurrences which attended Cuddeback and Gumaer at the time of their flight from France, and all in connection gives me reason to think that both of them resided in the capital mentioned.

Caudebec said that the vessel in which he escaped from his country had many wheat bread passengers on it, who, after a few days' sailing, began to complain of their fare on the vessel, and that they could not live on the diet furnished, when the same consisted of plenty of bread, meat, beans, and other vegetables, and such eatables as were generally had on ships, but were inferior to such as they had been habituated to. As for himself, he said he thought he could do well enough on such victuals, but, he said, before they arrived at their place of destination, provisions became scarce and they began to have good reason to complain. From which, it appears, that their voyage must have been retarded by contrary winds, or a circuitous route, to avoid being taken by their enemies. I have also understood that Gumaer lived in a city, and, when his enemies sought for him, he was reading in a garden, where he was informed of his enemies searching for him and he fled to the top of one of the houses, where he hid. Now,

HISTORY OF DEERPARK. 35

as it appears that this city was a flourishing place before it became reduced by the persecutions mentioned and suffered much in consequence of the same, and, as one of those two individuals bore the name of the town, it appears very probable that the passengers in the vessel mentioned were all from this capital.

I have been informed that Caudebec sometimes related the manner in which the Protestants, or Huguenots, were tortured and murdered, one of which I still remember, but consider it too shocking to our feelings to embrace it in this work, being worse, in my view, than the vile Nero's project of employing dogs to kill Christians. These innocent people in the early days of Christianity suffered great persecutions from those who were inimical to their professions and doctrines. It seems strange that after their doctrine became popular, the greatest proportion of those who embraced it in France became as cruel as the monster Nero, who had the power to exhibit to the world his thirst for imposing on mankind the numerous cruelties he caused to be inflicted. He became so destitute of the feelings of humanity that he caused even his own mother to be put to death to satisfy an unnatural curiosity. Also the great moralist, Seneca, who had been his tutor, did not escape his jealous disposition, but was put to death according to his orders. All his impositions for self present gratification will remain an everlasting stain on his character of the blackest dye, and the sufferings he caused to be endured must have affected thousands of his subjects.

Now, all these acts are only as a drop of water in a bucket to like acts unnecessarily imposed from time to time on the Roman people and other nations, by ruling characters of Roman dominions. What shall we think of mankind, who, for self-exaltation, have so overcome all those tender feelings implanted in their natures as to kill, murder and plunder each other without any just cause, but merely to satisfy the cravings of men who were a curse to the world? I do not know of any species of creatures on the globe who have acted as cruel as human beings have done in this respect. And by taking a view of the sins of the ancient nations, who have been destroyed, it appears that good reason existed for their destruction, and that all the animal tribes have yielded more to the government and laws of their Creator than mankind.

The name Gumaer, as now written, was on the certificate written "Guimar." In another writing, which gave Gumaer the right of citizenship in the English territories, it was written " Guymard." This writing was also found among the papers formerly of Peter Gumaer, jr., now (1858) in possession of his son-in-law, Solomon Van Etten, Esq. It is probable that the names Gomar, Guymard and Guimar, in France, originated from one of those names, the last of which is the name of a certain town within the French territories. I have never seen the handwriting of Cuddeback or Gumaer. The children of the first families were not educated, in consequence of which, when it became necessary to write their names in their business transactions, &c., the same was done in the Dutch tongue, without any other guide than that of the oral sound, which of the latter name had become somewhat broader among the Dutch than what it was originally ; and the French sound of " mar " was altered in the Dutch sound of " maer," which is the same as that of " maur " in the English tongue.

A hasty flight of these two individuals prevented them from being furnished with sufficient funds for a livelihood, in consequence of which it was concluded that two sisters of Cuddeback, who were to leave France afterwards and meet them at their place of destination (which, the writer has understood, was to be England, but it may have been in Holland), were to bring money for setting up a business of trade. It is probable that there was an intended marriage of Gumaer with one of those sisters. They did not arrive at the appointed time, and, after all hope of their coming was given up, these two young men embarked for America and landed in the State of Maryland, which passage exhausted all their money, and here they began to experience the want of it. After a short stay, they came into the State of New York, where both entered into a state of matrimony, Cuddeback with a daughter of Benjamin Provost, who was in a trading business either in the city of New York or somewhere in the vicinity of the Hudson river, whereby he became related to some Swartwout families, which probably led to an association of Cuddeback, the three Swartwouts and other companions to move into this part of the country. Peter, son of the first Gumaer, has said that his son Elias took after the Deyo family, which leads us to infer that Gumaer's wife was of a Deyo family.

The name of the father of the three Swartwouts is not known, but we have reason to believe it was

Gerardus, as this is a name which has been given to at least one member of each Swartwout generation from the first in this neighborhood to the present ; and also in the family of Harmanus Van Inwegen, whose wife was a Swartwout, and the name of their only son was Gerardus, which name has also continued in his family descendants to the present time. The name Jacobus (James) and the name Samuel, are Swartwout names, and have continued in those families to the present time. In the early part of the settlement here, there were two Swartwouts who sometimes came over here from the east side of the Hudson river (probably from Dutchess or Westchester counties) to see their relatives here. The name of one of them was Jacobus. (James), and he was generally called Dickke Jacobus (Thick James), in consequence of his bodily thickness. It was said he was uncommonly broad and thick around his shoulders and breast, and unusually strong. It is probable that the Swartwouts in this place either came from the city of New York or from one of the counties on the east side of the Hudson river, and that their ancestry emigrated from Holland into this country at an early period of its settlement for advancing their interests.

Cuddeback, Gumaer and one of the Swartwouts were the only three of the first settlers who remained in the present town of Deerpark, and they became the owners of the land granted by the patent; and having become too weak to defend their possessions against Jersey claimants, they let Harmanus Van Inwegen have some of their lands to come and reside here and help defend their possessions. He was a bold, strong and resolute man, on whom much reliance was placed. He was originally from Holland, and in the early part of his life had been a seafaring man. At a certain time he was at the house of Cuddeback, and on hearing him read that part of history which relates to Hindoo women suffering themselves to be burned, after the death of their husbands, in case of being the survivors, said that his own eyes had seen what he (Cuddeback) was reading, and mentioned the place of the occurrence and manner in which it was transacted. Van Inwegen had married a sister of the three Swartwouts.

It is somewhat uncertain which of the three Swartwouts remained in this neighborhood, but as the seats of Bernardus and Thomas became vacated, and Anthony's continued to be occupied by Van Inwegen, after Samuel and James Swartwout removed more distantly from the neighborhood first settled, I will make use of his name as the father of the two latter. Another reason is that the seats of Bernardus and Thomas became possessed by the second Peter Gumaer. He bought the rights of two Swartwouts.

It is not known what became of the families of Tyse and Jamison, nor where the two Swartwouts went, who removed from here. There are Swartwouts down the Delaware river, in the State of Pennsylvania, or New Jersey, among whom the name of Bernardus has been kept up. These probably are descendants of Bernardus who settled here. There also are Swartwouts on the Susquehanna. These may be descendants of Thomas Swartwout.

After the seven first settlers had resided here a few years, they sent Jacob Cuddeback to the Governor of the New York Colony to obtain a patent to cover as much land as they intended to occupy, which was granted the 14th of October, 1697, for 1,200 acres land to Jacob Cuddeback, Thomas Swartwout, Anthony Swartwout, Bernardus Swartwout, Jan Tyse, Peter Germar and David Jamison, who, as near as can be determined, continued to be the only settlers of white people in this part of the country for a term of more than 20 years. The strongest evidence of this is that the children of the first settlers between this place and the Delaware river were contemporary with the grandchildren of the first settlers, and that some of the children of the first pioneers were among the first settlers of both the lands between this place and the Delaware river, and a few miles down the same in the north part of New Jersey. One daughter of Jacob Cuddeback, one of Van Inwegen, one of Swartwout, and a sister of the second Peter Gumaer's wife, were among the first settlers between this place and the Delaware; and one son and four daughters of Cuddeback were among the first in the north of New Jersey.

There were two neighborhoods in this town, one of which, formerly known by the name of Peenpack neighborhood, extended southwest to the old county line, formerly between Orange and Ulster counties, and the other extended from that line southwest to the Delaware river, and was in the first instance designated " over the river neighborhood," in consequence of its population then being principally on the east side of the river, but after the increase of inhabitants on the west side of the river the whole district was generally termed " the lower neighborhood."

ANCIENT FAMILIES

OF THE

PEENPACK NEIGHBORHOOD.

FAMILY OF JACOB CUDDEBACK AND WIFE, MARGARET PROVOST—(Jacob Cuddeback lived to be about 100 years old.)

First son, Benjamin Cuddeback, never married. He, in the first instance, lived with his brother William, and afterwards with his nephew, Benjamin Cuddeback. (Lived to be about 80 years old.)

Second son, William Cuddeback, married Jemima Elting, daughter of ―――― Elting of the Old Paltz. He became owner of his father's farm, and resided on the premises afterwards occupied by his son, Captain Cuddeback. (Lived to be about 74 years old.)

Third son, James Cuddeback, married Neelje Decker, daughter of Christopher Decker, of Shipikunk, in the north part of New Jersey, where Cuddeback became a resident. (Died about 30 years of age.)

Fourth son, Abraham Cuddeback, married Esther Swartwout, daughter of Major James Swartwout, of Peenpack. They resided near the present dwelling house of Peter L. Gumaer until they became old and were removed by their sons to Skaneateles Lake, in this

State, where two of his sons lived. He owned a farm where he first resided. (Abraham Cuddeback died at Skaneateles Aug. 18th, 1796, aged 83 years. His wife died April 11th, 1798, aged 65.)

One daughter, Dinah Cuddeback, married Abraham Louw, a son of Tys Louw †, of Rochester, in Ulster county. He was a blacksmith and settled in Shipikunk, in the north part of New Jersey, and became owner of a good farm, of which Wilhemus Fredenburgh, Peter and Joseph Van Noy and James and Evart Van Auken afterwards became owners. (Dinah lived to be about 74 years old.)

Another daughter, Eleanor Cuddeback, married Evart Hornbeck, son of ———— Hornbeck, of Rochester, in Ulster county. They first settled on the

---

† Tys Louw and wife commenced life poor. The writer knows nothing respecting their ancestors. He was an indolent, non-providing and intemperate man. She was the reverse of him in those respects; and the whole business of the family devolved on her, in which he exercised no manner of control, but left the whole business of the family to be managed according to her direction. He was naturally good-natured, and very indulgent to her. She furnished him daily with such small portions of liquor as would not intoxicate him. She entered into the business of manufacturing linen, both for the wearing apparel of the family, and to defray the other expenses, and did yearly manufacture more than a supply for the same, the surplus of which she took to New York at the end of every year, and for it procured such articles of trade as her spinsters and neighbors generally wanted to purchase, and in this way she made a yearly addition to her stock of goods and thus obtained wealth and credit, so that she became enabled to keep a good assortment of such goods as were salable in her time and commanded quite an extensive trade. She also carried on the blacksmith business, for which she employed a workman and put her own son, Abraham Louw, with him in the shop to learn the trade. Not long before her decease she had told a confidential friend that she had ƒ1,200 in money. Besides this she had her store of goods and other property. The ƒ1,200 was equal to $3,000, which in her time was worth about three times as much as at the present time.

HISTORY OF DEERPARK. 43

farm now in possession of Joseph Cuddeback in this town, and afterwards moved into the neighborhood of Shipikunk, in New Jersey, and became residents on or near the premises lately occupied by his grandson, Capt. Benjamin Hornbeck, where they became owners of a good farm. He was a blacksmith, which was a good trade in his time. (Eleanor lived to be about 70 years.)

Another daughter, Else Cuddeback, married Harmanus Van Gorden, son of ———— ————. He was or became owner of the farm, which, after his death, was owned by his two sons, Daniel and Benjamin Van Gorden, in the neighborhood of Shipikunk. This name (Shipikunk) originated from the Indians, and probably had reference to the smooth rocks against the side of the mountain near the neighborhood, as the name "unk" is significant of rocks. (She lived to be about 80.)

Another daughter, Maria Cuddeback, married Geo. Westfall, son of ———— Westfall, of the neighborhood of Minnissing, in New Jersey. This was the ancient Indian name of the neighborhood in which the ancient Minisink church was located. Her husband died and she afterwards married ———— Cole. *

Youngest daughter, Naomi Cuddeback, married Lodiwyke Hornbeck, a widower, and son of Judge Jacob Hornbeck, of Rochester, in Ulster county, where

---
* This woman lived to a great age. It was said of her that in early life she became very fleshy and was taken with a severe sickness, which reduced her very low and she became lean, and having found the inconvenience of being fat and fleshy and fearing to become so again, she thereafter stinted herself in eating less than her appetite craved, and lived to the age of about 100 years. She had the reputation of a fine woman, possessed of excellent qualities of mind.

they continued to reside till after the decease of her husband, whom she survived, and underwent different scenes in life afterwards. She had the reputation of a sensible woman. They had one son named Henry and one daughter Maria. The former had children, but the latter had none. The writer knows nothing in relation to the children of Henry.

[There appears to have been another son of Jacob Cuddeback and Margaret Provost named Jacob, who was baptized in the Dutch church in New York, July 7th, 1706. His name is mentioned likewise in an old deed of his father. He married Jannetye Westbrook.]

SECOND GENERATION.

FAMILY OF WILLIAM CUDDEBACK AND JEMIMA ELTING.
(Married April 8th, 1732.)

First son, James Cuddeback, a very active young man, became deranged. (Lived to be about 80 years old.)

Second son, Abraham Cuddeback, married Esther Gumaer, daughter of the second Peter Gumaer. He remained in the homestead of his father and became owner of half of his real estate. He was Captain of a company of militia before and during the Revolutionary War. They had four sons, Col. William A. Cuddeback, Peter G. Cuddeback, Esq., Jacob Cuddeback and Cornelius Cuddeback, and two daughters—Esther, wife of Evart Hornbeck, and Jemima, wife of David Westfall. (Captain Abraham Cuddeback lived to be about 82 years old.)

Second son, Benjamin Cuddeback (lived to be about

45), married Catharine Van Fliet, daughter of John Van Fliet, of the lower neighborhood, in this town He became owner of the other half of his father's estate. They had four sons, William, Henry, Levi and Benjamin Cuddeback, Esq., and three daughters— Syntche, wife of Simon Westfall ; Jemima, wife of Anthony Van Etten. The other daughter died young, and Levi, after he became a young man, died suddenly of cholic.

Fourth son, Roulif Cuddeback (lived to be about 50 years old), never married. He fought the Indian, as mentioned in Eager's History. †

Only daughter, Sarah Cuddeback, married Daniel Van Fliet, son of John Van Fliet, of the lower neighborhood. They owned the farm heretofore sold by Samuel Cuddeback and William Donoldson to Ezekiel P. Gumaer and brothers (nearly one-half mile south of Port Clinton.) They had a son, Solomon, and a daughter, Sarah. (Mahakamack church records give the baptism of four more children—Mardochai, Willem, Thomas, Jacomyntje—1739, 1759.)

FAMILY OF JAMES CUDDEBACK AND WIFE, NEYLTJE DECKER.

An only son, James Cuddeback, married Neyltje Westbrook, daughter of —— Westbrook, who resided on the east side of Shawangunk mountain, in the northeast part of New Jersey. He, a poor man, by persevering industry became owner of a valuable farm.

---

† This was a hand-to-hand encounter with the Indian, near where Sol· Van Fleet now lives, in which neither were victors, and they parted, each glad to get away from the other.

He had three sons—John, James and Richard, and three daughters. Eleanor married Samuel Shelley, of Peppercotting (Papakating) valley, south of Deckertown, N. J.; Mary married Samuel Adams, of Deckertown; another daughter married James Wilson, of New Jersey. These sons all moved to Niagara county, N. Y., where their descendants are quite numerous. They spell their name Cudeback, using but one d.

FAMILY OF ABRAHAM CUDDEBACK AND WIFE, ESTHER SWARTWOUT.

First son, James Cuddeback, married Scynta Van Fliet, daughter of John Van Fliet, of the lower neighborhood.

Second son, Peter Cuddeback, married Margaret De Witt, daughter of Jacob R. De Witt, of this neighborhood.

Third son, Abraham Cuddeback, married Jane De Witt, also a daughter of J. R. De Witt. All the descendants of these sons are in Western New York, near Skaneateles.

Fourth son, Philip Cuddeback, never married. He died, when a young man, by over heating himself in seeking to stop a fire in the woods. (Mahackamack church records show the baptism of two daughters besides of Abraham Cuddeback—Annatje and Esther.)

FAMILY OF ABRAHAM LOUW AND DINAH CUDDEBACK, HIS WIFE. (Married May 31st, 1738.)

First daughter, Jane Louw, married Jacob Van Etten, son of John Van Etten, who resided near the

Delaware, in Pennsylvania or New Jersey. They became owners of tke Louw farm, in New Jersey. They had three daughters—Dinah, Margaret and Sarah, who became motherless soon after the birth of the last.

Second daughter, Naomi Louw, married Ezekiel Gumaer. (For their history refer to his name in advance.)

Third daughter, Margaret Louw, married Martin Westbrook, son of —————— Westbrook. He became owner of a farm in New Jersey, on which his daughter-in-law, Nancy Westbrook, now resides. They had one son, Abraham, and one daughter, Mary.

Fourth daughter, Sarah Louw, married Moses Depuy, son of Benjamin Depuy, Esq., of the Peenpack neighborhood. They had three sons—Benjamin, Abraham and Martin Depuy. The father was drowned in the Neversink river by falling from a raft at the close of the war.

By a second marriage with Jonathan Stanton, they had two sons—William and Moses Stanton. They owned a farm and resided on it, at the late residence of Harmanus Cuddeback, for some years, and exchanged it for a farm at Wurtsboro, of which the two sons became owners. (Mahackamack church records give the baptism of a son Jacobus ; baptized April 23, 1744.)

FAMILY OF EVART HORNBECK AND WIFE, ELEANOR CUDDEBACK.

First son, James Hornbeck, married Margaret Ennes, daughter of William Ennes. He became owner of a part of his father's farm. They had —————— sons,

namely, Evart, ——————————— and ————
daughters, namely (Elizabeth Ennes, baptized April 29, 1772, and Lena, born Dec. 23, 1780.)

Second son, Joseph Hornbeck, married Lydia Westbrook, daughter of Jacob Westbrook, of Shipikunk neighborhood. He became owner of a part of his father's farm. They had three sons and one daughter, Jacob, Benjamin and Saffrine (Severyne) and Lydia.

Third son, Benjamin Hornbeck, married Rebecca Wells, daughter of ——————— Wells. He died in early life. They had (two) sons, namely, (Joseph, baptized Oct. 29, 1780, and Jacobus, born Feb. 23, 1780), and ——————— daughters, namely, —————————————. Sara, bap. Nov. 25, 1776.

Fourth son, Evart Hornbeck, married Esther Cuddeback, daughter of Capt. Abraham Cuddeback. They occupied the farm now owned by Joseph Cuddeback. They had five sons—Joseph (bap. Feb. 16, 1785), Jacob, Abraham (bap. June 22, 1783), Benjamin and Cornelius, and two daughters—Eleanor and Jemima.

Daughters Maria Hornbeck married James Rosecrantz. They became owners of a good farm in Westfall township, in Pennsylvania. They had five daughters, namely, Betsy, wife of Manual Brink ; Lena, wife of Martyne Cole ; Catherine, whose first husband was Daniel Decker, and her second Crissie Bull ; Roanna, wife of Saunder (Alexander) Ennis ; Diana, wife of John B. Quick.

Daughter Margaret Hornbeck married Isaac Van Auken. They resided in the house afterwards occupied by their son, James Van Auken, and owned a farm of which his sons James and Evert Van Auken

HISTORY OF DEERPARK. 49

became possessed. They had three sons—Joseph (bap. Feb. 12, 1758), James (bap. April 8, 1764), and Evart, and three daughters, namely—(Seletie, bap. Oct. 17, 1773 ; Seletta, bap. Nov. 25, 1776 ; Grietje, bap. June 23, 1778.)

Daughter Lydia Hornbeck married John Westbrook, son of ———— Westbrook, of Minnissing, in New Jersey. They owned a good farm and had three daughters, one of whom died young. The names of the two surviving were Catharine, born July 15, 1767, and other records give the names of Jane, who married Levi Van Etten ; Maria, who married Cornelius Westbrook ; John I., who was blind ; Solomon, grandfather of John I. Westbrook, of present (1889) firm of Westbrook & Stoll ; Saffrein (Severyn), who married Blandina Westbrook.

Daughter Eleanor Hornbeck married Daniel Ennes, a blacksmith, and son of William Ennes. They had two sons—James and Alexander, and some daughters, namely,

He commenced with small means, and, by persevering industry, acquired a valuable property, viz : one farm, where his son Alexander resided, in New Jersey, and a farm in the vicinity of Owasco lake, in New York.

FAMILY OF HARMANUS VAN GORDEN AND WIFE, ELSIE CUDDEBACK. (Married June 11th, 1727.)

First son, Daniel Van Gorden, married Hannah Westbrook, daughter of Tjeick V. Westbrook, of a place now known by the name of Westbrookville. They had three or more sons—Levi,

Abraham, Martin (born Nov. 5, 1786), —— ——, and three or more daughters—Mary (bap. Oct. 17, 1773), Else (bap. June 14, 1775), Eleanor and Lena (bap. June 1, 1777.) He became owner of a part of his father's farm, on which they resided.

Second son, Benjamin Van Gorden, marred ——. He became owner of the other part of his father's farm. They had —— sons, namely, —— —— ——, —— —— ——, —— —— ——, and daughters, namely, —— ——, —— ——. One daughter, —— —— Van Gorden, married Wilhelmus Fredenburgh, of Shipikunk, where he became owner of a farm. They had five sons—Aaron, Benjamin, Daniel, Joshua and Hezekiah, and —— daughters, namely,

Aaron became the greatest historian of his time of the ancients in this valley within his vicinity.

FAMILY OF ANTHONY SWARTWOUT AND WIFE.

One son, Samuel Swartwout, married Esther Gumaer, daughter of Peter Gumaer. He owned the premises on which the writer now resides, and his house stood where the road from my house comes to the spring brook, which brook, in his time, was about 8 or 10 rods from the foot of the hill, and on the flat between the hill and brook some Indians continued to reside until the Revolutionary War commenced.

Another son, James (Jacobus) Swartwout, married Anne Gumaer, also a daughter of Peter Gumaer. He resided where Col. Peter P. Swartwout now resides, and became major of a regiment of militia, which extended over a wide district of territory in the present county of Orange.

One daughter, Jane Swartwout, married John (Jan) Van Fliet, who owned the farm now occupied by Michael and Solomon Van Fliet. †

FAMILY OF SAMUEL SWARTWOUT AND WIFE, ESTHER GUMAER.

The only daughter, Elizabeth Swartwout, married Benjamin Depuy, a son of Moses Depuy, of Rochester, in Ulster county. Depuy, after marriage, became a resident with his father-in-law and afterwards the owner of all his estate. He, after marriage, built, and, after the Revolutionary War ended, rebuilt the house of my present residence. He was for many years a Justice of the Peace; and, near the end of his life, removed to Owasco, where all his children, excepting one or two, had previously settled. They had five sons—Moses, Samuel, John, Benjamin and James, and three daughters—Margaret, Esther and Eleanor. His descendants are now all in western countries.

FAMILY OF MAJOR JAMES (JACOBUS) SWARTWOUT AND WIFE, ANNA GUMAER.

First son, Gerardus Swartwout, was killed by the Indians in the time of the French war in company with two soldiers, who also were killed at Westbrookville about five miles from Gumaer's fort.

Second son, Philip Swartwout, married Antje Wynkoop, a daughter of —— Wynkoop, of Rochester or its vicinity. He became owner of his father's estate,

---

† Now (1889) occupied by Solomon Van Fleet, a nephew of Michael and Solomon.

and resided at the present residence of Col. Swartwout. He was a Justice of the Peace before and in the beginning of the Revolutionary War, and one of the Committee of Safety. He was killed by the Indians when they invaded this neighborhood, and his two eldest sons were killed at the same time and another son was badly wounded. An Indian pursued his son James a half-mile across lots and fences, but could not overtake him. Swartwout and first wife had four sons—Gerardus (bap. Aug. 26, 1759), Philip, James (bap. Sept. 18, 1750), and Cornelius (bap. June 24, 1752.) (The Mahackamack church records give the baptism also of another son, Cornelius Wynkoop, bap. March 20, 1763), and one daughter, Anna (bap. June 17, 1754.) By a second marriage with Deborah Schoonover, he had one son, Peter Swartwout.

One daughter, Esther Swartwout, married Abraham Cuddeback, as has been mentioned. (For their history refer back to their names.)

Another daughter, Jane Swartwout, married ———— ————, of Rochester, Ulster Co.

Another daughter, ———— Swartwout, married ———— Durland, of the town of Warwick, in Orange county. There are many of their descendants in this county. They had ——— sons, namely, ————, ————, and ———— daughters, namely, ————, ————.

FAMILY OF JOHN (JAN) VAN FLIET AND WIFE, JANE SWARTWOUT.

One son, James (Jacobus) Van Fliet, married Margaret Palmatier. He became owner of his father's farm, now occupied by his sons, Michael and Solomon. They had four sons—John, Thomas, Michael (bap. Jan. 22, 1783), and Solomon, and ———— daughters, namely (Esyntje, baptized Oct. 29th, 1780 ; Elizabeth, born March, 1785 ; Clara.)

Another son, Daniel Van Fliet, married Sarah Cuddeback, of Peenpack. For their history refer back to their names.

Another son (Samuel, married Tjaetje Cole, married by J. C. Fryenmoet, Nov. 26th, 1752.) (See Mahackamack church records.)

One daughter, Deborah Van Fliet, married John Decker, who resided where Simon Westfall now lives, and owned the old Decker farm at that place and a farm east of Shawangunk mountain, which his sons, Levi and Isaiah, occupied after their father's decease. They had three sons—Levi (bap. Feb. 12, 1758), Isaiah and Isaac, and ———— daughters—Margery (born Aug. 31, 1768), Seletta (bap. Jan. 8, 1772.)

J. D.'s first wife, Elizabeth De Witt, was a daughter of Jacob De Witt, of Rochester.

Another daughter, Catharine Van Fliet, married Benjamin Cuddeback, son of William Cuddeback. For their history refer back to their names.

(The Mahackamack church records show the baptism of Marie, Oct. 23d, 1743, and another daughter, Marya, May 10th, 1747.)

FAMILY OF PETER GUIMAR AND WIFE, ESTHER.

A copy of his certificate of church membership in the French language, viz :

Nous, sonssequez ancien du consistoire, de Moire,

on l'absence de Monsieur Morin, nostre Ministre, certifions que Pierre Guimar, de ous on enui von fail, ei a tousjours fair profession de nostre religion, en laquelle il osesen sans commethe aveum scandalle qui soit venu a nostre connoissance qui empesche, quil re puisse estre admisula participation de nos Sacrements. En foy dequoy nons luy avons signele preveur certificon a Moire, ningtiesme 8 avril, 1686.

S. Avillaguer.
Losary Cillfand.

F. Guymard.

[TRANSLATION.]

We, the Elders of the ancient Church of Moire, in the absence of our minister, Mr. Morin, do certify that Peter Guimar, aged about 20 years, has made a profession of our religion, and that he has never (so far as we know) committed any act which should prevent him from the participation of our sacraments. In witness whereof we have signed the foregoing certificate, at Moire, the 20th day of April, 1686.

L. Avillaguer.
Losary Cillfand.

F Guymard.

[The above translation was made by Hulda Morris, daughter of Rev. Henry Morris.]

FAMILY OF PETER GUMAER AND WIFE, ESTHER.

Among the papers formerly in possession of Ezekiel Gumaer, was found a paper in the handwriting of Thomas Kyte, who formerly was a schoolmaster in the Peenpack neighborhood, which contain the dates of the births of the children of Peter Gumaer, in the Dutch tongue, of which the following is an abstracted copy, viz :

Dochter Anna was geboren de 30st Mart, 1693.
" Esther was geboren de 5d von May, in het yaer, 1697.
Dochter Ragel is geboren de 8st von February, in het yaer 1700.
Dochter Maria de 8st von December, in het yaer 1702.
" Elisabeth de 22st von Mart, in het yaer 1705.
Soon Peter de 15 de von November, in het yaer 1708.
This is in a different handwriting. { In het yaer 1710 is geboren Taitie De Wit, huys vrow von Peter Gumar, is geoverleden de 12d November, 1756.

[TRANSLATION.]

Daughter Anna was born the 30th March, in the year 1693.
Daughter Esther was born the 5th of May, in the year 1697.
Daughter Rachel was born the 8th of February, in the year 1700.
Daughter Mary the 8th of December, in the year 1702.
" Elizabeth the 22d of March, in the year 1705.
Son Peter the 15th of November, in the year 1708.
In the year 1710 was born Charity De Witt, wife of Peter Gumaer. She died the 12th November, 1756.

MARRIAGES, ETC., OF THE FIRST GENERATION.

One daughter, Esther Guimar, married Samul Swartwout, son of Anthony Swartwout. (For their history and of their descendants, refer back to their names.)

Another daughter, Anne Guimar, married James (Jacobus) Swartwout. (For their and descendants' history, refer back to their names.)

Another daughter, ———— Guimar, married Dubois, of Rochester, in Ulster county. He became a wealthy farmer. They had two daughters, namely, ———— and ————.

Another daughter, ———— Guimar, married Lodewyke, son of Judge Jacob Hornbeck, of Rochester. They had three sons—Isaac, Philip and Henry. After her death he married Naomi Cuddeback, as mentioned.

Another daughter (Mary) Guimar, married (Jan) Elting, of Old Shawangunk, where he occupied a farm. They had one son, Peter.

One only son, Peter Guimar, married Charity De Witt, daughter of Jacob De Witt, of Rochester. He became owner of all his father's real estate, excepting what was granted to Samuel and James Swartwout. It was said the father gave a good portion to each of his daughters for that time. About two or three years before the French war commenced, Peter Guimar built a stone house (see page 29), 40x45 feet on the ground, a cellar under the whole, and a high, roomy chamber above the upper floor. Along two sides, below the eaves of the roof, were made port-holes through which to shoot, either when the house was built or the war commenced. This was a lucky transaction for himself and neighbors. It was the largest house in this part of the country, and best location in this neighborhood for a fort ; and when the French war commenced, a picket fort was erected on its front and rear sides, and all the families of the neighborhood moved into it, excepting those women and children who were sent to their relatives in Rochester, Old Paltz and other places. A barn, which the father had built, was 50 by 60 feet on the ground, its floor 30 by 60 feet, a stable on each side 60 feet long. This was an additional advantage.

SECOND GENERATION.

FAMILY OF THE SECOND PETER GUMAER AND WIFE, CHARITY DE WITT.

In his time the family name began to be written " Gumaer," and has continued to be so written by his descendants, and that orthography now used will from hence be continued.

The following is an abridged copy of the last part of the Dutch record heretofore mentioned, to wit:
Dochter Esther geboren de 2d January, 1729-30.
Soon Peter geboren de 19 February, 1731.
Dochter Maregretj geboren de 12de van Mey, 1736.
Soon Jacob De Witt geboren de 12de van December, 1739.
Soon Ezekiel geboren de 29st van December, 1742.
Dochter Maria geboren de 16de van July, 1745.
Soon Elias geboren de 22st van January, 1748.
Dochter Elizabeth geboren de 5de van November, 1750. Sye was overladen de 2de van July, 1752.

[TRANSLATION.]

Daughter Esther born the 2d January, 1729-30.
Son Peter born the 19th February, 1731.
Daughter Margaret born the 12th of May, 1736.
Son Jacob De Witt born the 12th of December, 1739.

Son Ezekiel born the 29th of December, 1742.
Daughter Mary born the 16th of July, 1745.
Son Elias born the 22d of January, 1748.
Daughter Elizabeth born the 5th of November, 1750. She died the 2d of July, 1752.

Oldest daughter, Esther Gumaer, married Abraham Cuddeback. For their and descendants' history, refer back to their names.

Oldest son, Peter Gumaer, married Hannah Van Inwegen, daughter of Gerardus Van Inwegen. He became owner of a part of his father's estate, on which he lived during his life. They had three sons—Jacob, Gerardus and Peter, and one daughter Elizabeth.

Daughter Margaret Gumaer married John Decker, son of Thomas Decker. He became owner of the farm now occupied by George Cuddeback † and resided on it during his life. They had one or more children, and she and they died. He afterwards married Sarah Hornbeck.

Son Jacob De Witt Gumaer married Hulda Decker, daughter of Thomas Decker, of the lower neighborhood. He became owner of a part of his father's estate and resided on it at the present residence of Solomon Van Etten, Esq. ‡. They had two sons—Peter and Jacob D. Gumaer, and six daughters—Jane, Hannah, Elizabeth, Esther, Mary and Charity.

Son Ezekiel Gumaer married Naomi Louw, daughter of Abraham Louw, of Shipikunk, in New Jersey. He remained in the homestead of his father and owned a

---

† Now (1889) occupied by Henry Cuddeback.
‡ Now (1889) occupied by Cornelius Caskey.

part of his farm. They had two sons—Peter E. and Abraham. The latter died when a small boy.

Daughter Mary Gumaer married James Devens. They became owners of the old Devens' farm in Mamakating, on which they continued to reside during their lives. They had five sons—Elias, Jacob, Peter, James and Abraham, and one daughter Charity.

Youngest son, Elias Gumaer, married Margaret Depuy, daughter of Benjamin Depuy, Esq., of this neighborhood. He first had a farm of his father, on which he resided for some years. This he exchanged for the farm on which he last resided and sold to Abraham Cuddeback, Esq. He and his wife, in their old age, removed to the western part of New York, where their children had previously settled. They had four sons—Benjamin, Elias, Samuel and Peter E. Gumaer, and two daughters—Charity and Elizabeth.

FIRST GENERATION.

FAMILY OF HARMANUS VAN INWEGEN AND WIFE, ———— SWARTWOUT.

His son, Gerardus Van Inwegen, married Jane De Witt, daughter of Jacob De Witt, of Rochester, in Ulster county. He became owner of his father's farm and resided where his son Cornelius lived previous to his removal from this neighborhood.

His daughter, Hannah Van Inwegen, married Thos. Decker. He was or became owner of the present farm of George Cuddeback, and resided at his present residence. (Now, 1889, occupied by Henry Cuddeback.)

SECOND GENERATION.

FAMILY OF GERARDUS VAN INWEGEN AND WIFE, JANE DE WITT.

First son, Harmanus Van Inwegen, married Margaret Cole, daughter of David Cole. He became owner of the farm now of Col. Peter Cuddeback, and resided near his present dwelling house. He was a Justice of the Peace for some years in and after the Revolutionary War, and also one of the Committee of Safety in that war. They had eight sons—Gerardus, David, Cornelius, Jacob, Samuel, Jacob and Josias, and two daughters—Charlotte and Hannah. Gerardus was killed or taken prisoner at Fort Montgomery, when it was taken, and the first Jacob died when about 12 or 14 years old of a short illness.

Second son, Jacob Van Inwegen, never married. He owned a part of his father's estate, which, after his death, became the property of his two brothers. He resided with his brother Harmanus until the end of his life.

Third son, Cornelius Van Inwegen, married Eleanor Westbrook, daughter of Terrick V. Westbrook, of now Westbrookville, in Ulster county (now Sullivan county, 1889.) He continued to reside on the homestead of his father, and became owner of that part of his father's farm. They removed, in their old age, into the western part of this State, where nearly all their children had previously settled. They had nine sons— Abraham, Gerardus, Daniel, John, Jacob, Levi, Cornelius, Henry and Martin, and one daughter Mary. Cornelius, the seventh son, died when a child, and Martin was killed by lightning in driving a wagon from a hay-stack towards home in time of haying. Both horses driven by him were also killed.

One daughter, Margaret Van Inwegen, married John Wallace. They resided in this town until a few years after the Revolutionary War, when they removed to Onondagua, in this State. They had one son Cornelius and one daughter Jane.

Another daughter, Hannah Van Inwegen, married Peter Gumaer, as mentioned. (For their history refer back to their names.)

The descendants of this last family have all moved into Pennsylvania, New Jersey and the western part of New York.

(Kingston church records show the baptism of another daughter Jenneke, Feb. 2d, 1735, and Mahackamack church records those of Tjaade, May 30th, 1739, and Elizabeth, March 15th, 1747.)

SECOND GENERATION.

FAMILY OF THOMAS DECKER AND HANNAH VAN INWEGEN.

First son, Daniel Decker, married ―――― ――――. They settled in New Jersey, some distance down the

Delaware river, where he owned a farm. They had —— sons, ———, ———, ———, ———, and —— daughters, ———, ———.

Second son, John Decker, first married Margaret Gumaer; for their history refer back to their names, and afterwards Sarah Hornbeck, daughter of Benjamin Hornbeck, of Rochester, They had two sons— Benjamin and Daniel, and four daughters Margaret, Jane, Hannah and Mary. At the commencement of the Revolutionary War, he became Major of a Regiment of Militia of Orange county, and, when the Indians invaded the lower neighborhood, he was wounded by the enemy, on his return from a funeral, and narrowly escaped from being taken.

Third son, Peter Decker, married (Catrina) Cole. They resided in the north part of New Jersey, and had two sons Thomas and John, and ——— daughters— Sarah (bap. July 24, 1763), Jane.

First daughter, Hannah Decker, married Anthony Van Etten, son of ——— Van Etten, of Rochester, or its vicinity. He obtained a piece of land of his father-in-law and built the house afterwards occupied by his son, Henry Van Etten, on which he also erected a blacksmith shop, and with the help of an apprentice pursued the blacksmith business, of which he obtained a great run and became owner of one of the best farms in the present town of Deerpark. He served some years as a Justice of the Peace. They had ——— sons—Levi (bap. Feb. 12, 1758), Henry, Thomas (bap. Sept. 8, 1751), Anthony. (The Mahackamack church records gives the baptism of other children, namely: Antje, bap. Jan. 14, 1753 ; Jenneke, bap. Ap. 28, 1754 ; Margrieta, bap. Feb. 13, 1756 ; Alida, bap. Aug. 19, 1759 ; Blandina, bap. Sept. 4, 1763 ; Maria, bap. Nov. 2, 1765 ; Tomas, bap. October 16, 1768 ; Jacob, Oct. 29, 1770), and —— daughters.

Second daughter, Hulda Decker, married Jacob De Witt Gumaer. (For their history refer back to their names.)

The descendants of those four ancient families are dispersed into different parts of our country, and have become settled in different parts of New York, New Jersey, Pennsylvania, Ohio, Michigan, Wisconsin, California, and probably in some other States and territories ; and some, in connection with those among whom they have intermarried, have remained on the premises of their forefathers and now possess nearly all the valuable land for agricultural purposes in the present town of Deerpark.

The reader will learn from this history that generally the descendants of the first pioneers became farmers, and continued in those occupations to the end of the third generation ; and the greatest proportion of the fourth and fifth generation of the present time (1858) are farmers. Our ancestors were not in opulent circumstances, but generally had a plenty of the necessaries of life and were a thriving people, and, so far as the writer's knowledge extends in relation to those who have settled in other parts of our country, they have generally acquired farms.

Jacob Cuddeback has been known to say that by leaving France he had been deprived of many enjoyments he might have had in that country, but for these sacrifices he had the satisfaction of leaving his posterity in a country of good land and easily to be acquired.

It appears that the first emigrants craved title for no more land than what they wanted to occupy, thinking that the mountainous land bordering on it would remain unsold, and that they and their descendants could always get wood from it without paying for the land. This continued so for about sixty or seventy years, when they had to buy it at a higher price than they felt willing to pay for it, for a supply of fuel, fencing, timber, &c. The patentees now saw their mistake, and Jacob Cuddeback at a certain time was censured by his son William for not having included land enough in the patent to cover an additional tract of wood land. The old man, not relishing this, replied, " We all can see the mistake now, when it is too late. You have the same chance I had to provide for your family. See if you will do better."

The descendants of the four pioneers have generally acquired as much territory as was necessary to obtain by the sweat of the brow comfortable livings for their respective families; and not only have they obtained a competency for their livelihood, but a large surplus, which, as the avails of it, have reached all branches of mechanical and other business whatever in our country; and many of their productions, together with the masses of other producers, have been conveyed to European countries. In consequence of which they have been valuable citizens, and have rendered extensive benefits to mankind, from whom, in return, they have received an equal amount of necessary articles and luxuries. The whole annual surplus amount now produced by the fourth and fifth generations of the ancient little neighborhood of Peenpack, must amount in value to many thousands of dollars.

FAMILY OF JACOB R. DE WITT AND WIFE, JANE DEPUY.

They removed from Neponaugh (Napanock), in Ulster county, into the neighborhood of Peenpack about the year 1760. He was a son of Egbert De Witt, of the former place, and she was a daughter of Moses Depuy, of Rochester. He built the old stone and frame house at the Neversink river, and a grist mill near the present aqueduct across the river, and owned the farm he formerly occupied, together with those premises. In the commencement of the Revolutionary War a fort was built contiguous to his house, which has been termed Fort De Witt †, and he was commissioned Captain of a Company of Rangers for guarding this frontier. According to Eager's History, it is satisfactorily ascertained that De Witt Clinton was born in this house. The writer has also been informed by a near neighbor, formerly of the Clinton family, that he was born at that place.

The family of Jacob R. De Witt and wife consisted of three sons—Moses (bap. Dec. 12, 1766), Egbert and

---

† Fort De Witt was located near the Suspension Bridge which crosses the Neversink river, on the road leading from Port Jervis to Cuddebackville, about one mile south of Cuddebackville. The small house standing (1889) near the present dwelling of Jesse Tillson, is on the foundation of this fort.

Jacob, and seven daughters—Mary, Rachel, ———
Margaret, Jane, Hannah and Esther.

Moses had a suitable genius for obtaining scientific knowledge, and an uncommon relish for the same; he also was naturally a very persevering student and of an amiable disposition. His opportunities for obtaining education were small; but he acquired much in view of the disadvantages under which he labored, and far beyond that of any of his contemporaries in this part of our country who had the same opportunities with himself. He became employed as one of the under-surveyors to run the line between the State of New York and Pennsylvania, and afterwards one of the Surveyors to survey the military lands in the State of New York. He died about the age of 27 years, possessed of a very valuable property of unsettled lands in the district of military lands in this State. He and his brother Egbert both died unmarried.

Youngest son, Jacob, removed from this neighborhood before he arrived to manhood.

Daughter Mary De Witt married William Rose, from Little Britain or its vicinity. In the time of the Revolutionary War he was commissioned a Captain to inlist a company of soldiers to serve in that war, and, after it ended, he became Captain of a company of militia. He, in the latter part of his life, owned the farm, mill, &c., of his father-in-law, then deceased.

Daughter Rachel De Witt married Robert Burnet, of Little Britain, where he owned and occupied a farm. He has served in different county and State offices.

One daughter married ——————— ——————— ;

daughters Margaret and Jane married Cuddeback, as has been mentioned. (For their history refer back to their names.)

Daughter Hannah De Witt married James Ennes, son of Daniel Ennes, of New Jersey. They became owners of a farm near the outlet of Skaneateles lake.

Daughter Esther De Witt married James Depuy, son of Benjamin Depuy, Esq., of the Peenpack neighborhood. They settled at Onondaga, where they owned and occupied a farm. He served in civil and military offices.

Abraham Westfall and wife, Blandina Van Etten, became residents in the southwest end of the Peenpack neighborhood, in the latter part of the Revolutionary War, and he became owner of a small, ancient Westfall farm, now included in the farm occupied by Capt. Henry Swartwout. A few rods east of his dwelling house stood the old stone house of Westfall. This was the house where the fort was in the time of the French war, and which the Indians attacked and killed part of a company of soldiers who were traveling from New Jersey to Esopus, and, just before the attack, had stopped in to rest and take refreshments. The particulars of this are stated in Eager's History of Orange County.

Abraham Westfall was a son of ——— Westfall, and his wife was a daughter of Anthony Van Etten, Esq., of the lower neighborhood. In the latter part of the Revolutionary War, Westfall was commissioned a Captain of the soldiers, who, from time to time, were stationed on this frontier. Near the end of the war he built a small fort at his house, and, with a few soldiers and one or two families, occupied the same. Sometime after the war ended, he removed with his family to one of the Southern States.

(Children, Joseph, baptized Aug. 18th, 1782; Annatje, baptized April 20th, 1784. Mahackamack church records.)

FAMILY OF JAMES DAVIS AND WIFE, ELIZABETH KATER.

They removed from the lower neighborhood into the Peenpack neighborhood soon after the Revolutionary War ended. She was originally from Rochester or its vicinity. They had three sons—Solomon, James and Daniel, and —— daughters—Leah, Elizabeth, Anna, —— and Polly. They all removed into the western part of this State, excepting some of the daughters.

FAMILY OF WILLIAM GEEGGE AND WIFE, LEAH DAVIS.

He was originally from Ireland and by trade a millwright. His wife was a daughter of James Davis, father of the preceding family. They were married a few years after the Revolutionary War ended. He built and occupied a grist-mill on a farm he purchased. The mill seat and farm is now owned by John Van Etten, Esq. They had one son, William, and a daughter.

There were a few other families in the vicinity of the Peenback neighborhood.

ANCIENT FAMILIES
OF THE LOWER NEIGHBORHOOD.

The following were ancient families who resided in the lower neighborhood of this town, who, as near as

HISTORY OF DEERPARK.   69

can be ascertained, must have commenced to settle in the same more than 20 years after the first settlement was made at Peenpack :

FAMILY OF HENRY CORTRIGHT AND WIFE, MARGARET DECKER.

She probably was a sister of Thomas Decker. He must have been from Rochester. They resided where Aaron Whitlock now lives, and became owners of his present farm.

One son, Daniel Cortright (bap. May 3, 1743), married ——— ———. They first resided on the east side of Shawangunk mountain, in the town of Minisink, and from thence removed into the western part of York State. They had —— sons, ——— ———, and —— daughters.

Another son, Moses Cortright (bap. March 24, 1745), married ——— Van Etten, daughter of Anthony Van Etten, Esq. They continued to reside in the house of his father, and he became owner of his homestead farm. A few years after the Revolutionary War ended, he with his family removed into the western part of this State. They had —— sons, namely, ———, ———, and —— daughters.

FAMILY OF ABRAHAM VAN AUKEN AND WIFE.

They resided between the present residences of David Swartwout and Joseph Cuddeback, where he owned a farm. They had three sons—Cornelius, Josias and Abraham. They, or two of them, moved into the western part of this State soon after it began to be settled. They had —— daughters, namely— ———— , ———— .

FAMILY OF JOHN WESTBROOK AND WIFE, MAGDELENA WESTBROOK.

He owned the farms now of Abraham J. and Isaac Cuddeback, and resided where the old house of the former now stands, in a stone house. He for some years kept a small store for Indian trade and a tavern. He was Captain of a company of militia. He had (six) sons, namely—(Anthonie, bap. Oct. 31, 1738 ; Johannes, bap. Sept. 19, 1740 ; Johannes, bap. Nov. 16, 1746 ; Samuel, bap. March 12, 1749 ; Joel, bap. April 11, 1756 ; Gideon, bap. Nov. 21, 1759), and (four) daughters, namely—(Autje, bap. Dec. 23, 1744 ; Alida, bap. June 21, 1747 ; Elizabeth, bap. March 24, 1751 ; Sara, bap. June 17, 1753.) Nearly all his descendants have removed from this place.

FAMILIES OF VAN AUKEN—HENRY DECKER,

And another individual were early settlers on the farm heretofore occupied by Benjamin Cuddeback, Esq., now by his sons, Elting and Dr. Thomas Cuddeback. Van Auken resided at the former residence of Jacob Shimer, Decker where Elting now resides, and the other near the mouth of the brook. The two latter had grist-mills. None of their descendants have remained in this town. The wife of Jacob Shimer was a daughter or grandaughter of Van Auken. They had one son, Richard, who married a daughter of Daniel Ennes, and two daughters, one of whom married Hezekiah Fredenburgh, and the other ——— ————. They, all of this family, removed into the western part of this State.

FAMILY OF JAMES VAN AUKEN AND WIFE,

Settled at the present residence of James D. Swartwout, Esq., and owned his farm. He was the first Justice of the Peace in the present town of Deerparkt which office he probably derived from the governmen, of the State of New Jersey. He was a brother of Van Auken mentioned.

His son, Daniel Van Auken, married Leah Kettle, daughter of ——— ————. He became owner of his father's farm, and occupant of his house, at which a fort was built in the time of the Revolutionary War ; and when the Indians invaded this neighborhood, they attacked the fort and two Indians were shot. They shot old James Van Auken as he looked through a window on the chamber. They had ——— sons—Elijah, Nathaniel, Nathan, Absolum, Joshua, Daniel, Jeremiah, ———, and ——— daughters, namely, ———, ———, ———, ———, ———, ———, whole number fifteen. One of his sons, a school teacher, was killed by the Indians when they invaded the lower neighborhood. These descendants became dispersed into different parts of our country.

SOLOMON KUYKENDALL AND WIFE, SARAH COLE,

Resided at the present residence of the widow Elting and her family, and owned their present farm. He was a Justice of the Peace in the time of the Revolutionary War and after it ended. James Van Fliet, jr., became owner of his real estate. From which I infer that the former had no children living at the time of his decease. Van Fliet had two sons—Solomon, who married a daughter of Benjamin Carpenter, and the other, Daniel, married a daughter of Jacob Westbrook.

Van Fliet, after some years' occupation of the premises, sold and removed with his family west into Pennsylvania or York State.

FAMILY OF SIMON WESTFALL AND WIFE, JANE (JANNETJE) WESTBROOK.

They resided in the old stone house now or lately occupied by James Bennet, Esq. He owned a gristmill there and some land. They had (eight) sons— Simeon (bap. Feb. 12, 1749) ; Wilhelmus (bap. July 8, 1753) ; John De Witt (bap. May 19, 1751) ; Jury (bap. April 23, 1744) ; Jury (bap. Jan. 24, 1748) ; Solomon (bap. Jan. 27, 1759) ; Daniel (bap. June 5, 1763), and Reuben (bap. April 8, 1764.) Also (three) daughters, namely—Aeltje (bap. Oct. 6, 1745) ; Aeltje (bap. Feb. 1756), and Blandina (bap. Nov. 9, 1760.) Wilhelmus

HISTORY OF DEERPARK. 73

settled east of the Shawangunk mountain, near Deckertown, in the State of New Jersey.

His son, Simeon Westfall, married Sarah Cole, daughter of David Cole. They became residents in the old stone house at Port Jervis, in Pennsylvania, where he had a good farm, now possessed by different occupants, Samuel Fowler, Simeon Westfall, Dimmick and others. Westfall and wife had three sons, Simon (bap. Feb. 9, 1766), David and George, and two daughters, Jane and ———.

Son John D. Westfall married Mary Davis, daughter of Samuel Davis. They resided in the stone house now occupied by (David) Westfall, in the Clove, in the north part of New Jersey, where he became owner of a good farm. They had ——— sons, Samuel De Witt Westfall (bap. Oct. 29, 1780), ———, ———.

They all removed into the western part of York State.

Son Reuben Westfall married (Tjaetje) Kuykendall, daughter of Jacob Kuykendall. They remained in the old homestead and he remained in possession of the farm and mill of his father. They had ——— daughters, ———, ———.

One daughter (Blandina) Westfall, married John Brink. They and family have moved into western countries. (The Mahackamack church records contain the baptism of two children—Femmetje, Oct. 29, 1780 ; Reuben Westfall, April 22, 1784.)

FAMILY OF WILLIAM COLE AND WIFE.

They settled near the present dwelling house of Eli Van Inwegen, Esq., and owned a farm there.

His son, Wilhelmus Cole, married Leah Westbrook, daughter of Cornelius Westbrook, of Jersey State. He occupied the house of his father until he built a new one after the war ended at the same place ; and owned his father's farm. They had two sons—Josias (bap. Nov. 21, 1764), and Cornelius Westbrook Cole (bap. Feb. 7, 1767), and two daughters—Maria, (bap. Oct. 16, 1772), ———.

Solomon Decker, from Old Shawangunk, and wife, Eleanor Quick, daughter of ——— Quick, an early resident of the present township of Westfall, in Pennsylvania, settled with their family in the lower neighborhood in the time of the Revolutionary War, near the present residence of David Swartwout*. They had seven sons—Solomon (bap. Feb. 9, 1746), Jacob (bap. Sept. 13, 1761), Thomas (bap. Aug. 19, 1759), James (bap. Feb. 2, 1752), Joseph (bap. July 4, 1756), Peter (bap. June 21, 1767), and Isaac M. Decker, and three daughters—Margaret (bap. April 14, 1754), Lydia (bap. Oct. 11, 1747), and Mary (bap. March 4, 1750.) None of this family have remained in the present town of Deerpark. Youngest son, Isaac M. Decker, is yet living and now in 1859 is 92 years old.

FAMILY OF PETER KUYKENDALL AND WIFE, FAMITJE DECKER.

They resided in now Port Jervis, where Elias Kuykendall formerly lived, and he was owner of a farm there ; all, or nearly all, of which is now covered by the Village of Port Jervis. (The Kingston church

---

* Now (1889) the residence of Peter D. Swartwout.

book records the baptism of a son, Martinas, June 18, 1734, and the Mahackamack records that of Jacob, Aug. 23, 1737, and a second Jacob, Oct. 30, 1739.)

Son Peter Kuykendall married (Catharina) Kettel. He continued to live with his father and became owner of his farm. They had four sons—Wilhelmus, Martin (bap. April 8, 1764), Solomon (bap. Oct. 21, 1753), and Elias, and (three) daughters, namely—Elizabeth (bap. June 19, 1757), Christyntje, (bap. Aug. 26, 1759), and Lea (bap. Dec. 8, 1765.) Their descendants are dispersed into different parts of our country.

FAMILY OF JOHN DECKER AND WIFE.

He owned an extensive farm or tract of land along the Delaware river, the southeast part of which bounded on the land of Kuykendall, near which he probably first settled †.

---

† It is now a few years over a century since the fall of the deepest snow ever known in this part of our country; and before it fell Peter Kuykendall and wife went to Esopus and left their children home, where John Decker and his wife were to go daily and see to them and render such assistance as would be necessary. Two or three days after they started this snow fell, and the morning after its falling John Decker commenced to shovel and make a footpath through the snow to Kuykendall's house. He worked all that day and the greatest part of the next day before he got to it, and found the door shut so that the children could not get out of the house. The door opened to the outside, and the snow laid so deep against it that it could not be opened from the inside before the snow was removed. It is probable that they first settled as near to each other as their situations of ground, water, &c., would admit. No victuals had been prepared for the children on the previous day to serve them for the next. They contrived to get meal, mix it up with water, bake it some on the hearth before the fire, and lived on it till they were otherwise provided for.

One son, Martin Decker, married ———— ————
They lived in the old stone house of Stephen St. John, and he became owner of a part of his father's farm. They had two sons—John and Richard, and ———— daughter, ————.

FAMILY OF SOLOMON DAVIS AND WIFE, LEAH DECKER.

They resided near the present grist-mill of Thomas Van Etten, Esq., and he owned a grist-mill at that place. They had —— sons—James, Daniel, Joel, ————, and —— daughters—Beletje, ————. (The following is the baptismal record of the children of Solomon Davis and Leah Decker : Kingston records—Lea, March 26, 1735 ; Jacobus, May 18, 1736. Mahackamack records—Beletje, May 31, 1738 ; Daniel, June 18, 1740 ; Joel, April 23, 1744 ; Jonas, June 16, 1745 ; Catharina, June 21, 1747 ; Elizabeth, Jan. 20, 1748 ; Petrus, April 15, 1750 ; Salomon, April 5, 1752.)

Oldest son, James Davis, married Elizabeth Kater. For their history refer back to their names.

Second son, Daniel Davis, was the strongest man of his time in the present town of Deerpark.

FAMILIES OF ———— WESTFALL AND DAVID COLE

were the first settlers on the present farms of Levi and Thomas Van Etten, Esq.

George Davis and wife, Deborah Schoonnover, had one son, Samuel, who became owner of the ancient grist-mill at T. Van Etten's mill seat.

Very little is now known respecting these four last mentioned ancient families.

Some of the families in the lower neighborhood, who, by marriages had become connected with certain families in the Peenpack neighborhood, are included in the history of the latter and here omitted.

It will be seen by this history of the ancient citizens of the lower neighborhood that they, as well as the others mentioned, were farmers, and they have also obtained their livings by the cultivation of the earth (a laborer's business), and not only provided a competency for their respective families, but also a surplus for the markets of our country to support those in other pursuits of life; but there now are of the present generations of the descendants of both neighborhoods some in nearly all the different occupations of life in our country.

From the length of time which intervened between the first settlement nearest at Peenpack and that made in the lower neighborhood, it appears probable that the latter was prevented by the Indian chief who resided on the land now of Levi or Thomas Van Etten, Esq.

LONGEVITY OF THE FIRST AND SECOND GENERATIONS.

The ages to which the first and second generations arrived, cannot all be correctly ascertained for want of records of the times of their several births and deaths. The only record of which the writer is in possession, is that of the families of the first and second Peter Gumaer, relative to the births of their respective children. These two records are a guide to get into the neighborhood of the times of the births of the members of the other families, and from what I have obtained from inscriptions on tombstones and the information I have had relative to the times to which some of them lived, I can correctly determine the ages of some of them and within a few years of others.

It was said of Jacob Cuddeback, by his grandson, Capt. Cuddeback, that he lived to the age of 100 years and retained his faculties good to the end of his life. In 1686, when Peter Gumaer was 20 years old, and he and Cuddeback had to leave France, the latter cannot have been less than 20 or 25 years of age. It appears he lived until after the inhabitants of this neighborhood had to buy some land out of Expense lot number two, in the Minisink patent, for a supply of fuel, rail timber, &c., which must have been about the year 1766. From all of which it appears that the age of Cuddeback cannot have been less than 100 years, and that the answer he made to his son William, heretofore mentioned, near the end of his life, shows that his intellect was yet good at that time.

AGES OF FIRST GENERATION.

FAMILY OF JACOB CUDDEBACK.

		Years.
Himself..		100
His sons. { Benjamin..............................	about	80
William.................................	"	74
James....................................	"	30
Abraham...............................	"	80
His wife, Esther Swartwout..............	"	80
Daughters { Maria....................................	"	100
Dinah.....................................	"	74
Eleanor..................................	"	70
Else..	"	70
Naomi....................................	"	80

AGES OF THE SECOND GENERATION.

FAMILY OF WILLIAM CUDDEBACK.

Sons. { 1st. James................................	about	80
2d. Abraham..........................	"	82
3d. Benjamin..........................	"	45
4th. Roolif (*premature*)............	"	50
Only daughter Sarah...........................	"	70

These are all the descendants of the ancient Cuddeback family who remained in the present town of Deerpark.

FIRST GENERATION.

FAMILY OF ANTHONY SWARTWOUT.

His sons { Samuel Swartwout................about 70
James Swartwout (premature)...... " 63
One daughter, wife of John Van Fliet......Unknown.

SECOND GENERATION.

FAMILY OF SAMUEL SWARTWOUT.

Years.
One only daughter, Elizabeth............about 60
Her husband, Benjamin Depuy............ " 80

FAMILY OF JAMES SWARTWOUT.

Anne Gumaer, his first wife..............about 50
His second wife, Anna Westbrook......... " 90
Son Philip Swartwout (premature)........ " 51
His wife, Deborah....................... " 60
His son, James Swartwout................ " 90
And wife, Jane Hornbeck .... " 90

These two last individuals were contemporary with the second generation, though James was of the next descent.

FIRST GENERATION.

FAMILY OF PETER GUMAER.

It is not known to what ages his five daughters arrived, but none of them became old. They all lived till after married and had children. Two of them had each one child, one had two, another three, and the other four. All their husbands became widowers, and two or more of them had second wives. It is probable that they all died between the ages of 30 and 60 years. It was said that in the days of their youth they labored very hard, both on the farm and to manufacture their cloth and do their housework, and yet had a delicate appearance and very fair skin. It was said of one of them that she would plough a whole week and become very dirty, and on Sunday wash and clean herself and put on clean clothes and appear in their reading meetings with skin as fair and white as that of any lady who was kept housed out of the sun's influence. Peter Gumaer, their brother, is the only one of the family I have seen. He also was a fair complexioned man. It was said that the ancient Cuddebacks were also fair complexioned, and that Major Swartwout and his sons, Esqs. Swartwout, were not only fair complexioned, but large and very fine, portly men when young in prime of life, and that the appearance of the Major on military parades was dignified and noble.

Years.
Age of Peter Gumaer.................... 71

SECOND GENERATION.

FAMILY OF THE SECOND PETER GUMAER.

Years.
1st daughter, Esther Gumaer..............about 70
Son Peter................................... "   85
Daughter Margaret........................... "   30

	Years.
Son Jacob D.	92
His wife, Huldah Decker.	" 75
Son Ezekiel.	80
His wife, Naomi Louw.	84
Daughter Mary.	" 80
Her husband, James Devens.	" 70
Son Elias.	" 70
His wife, Margaret Depuy.	" 70

FIRST GENERATION.

FAMILY OF HARMANUS VAN INWEGEN.

	Years.
His son, Gerardus.	about 90
Daughter Hannah.	" 80
Ages of the wife and husband.	Unknown.

SECOND GENERATION.

FAMILY OF GERARDUS VAN INWEGEN.

	Years.
First son, Harmanus.	about 80
His wife, Margaret Cole.	" 85
Son Jacob.	" 70
Son Cornelius.	" 80
His wife, Eleanor Westbrook.	Unknown.

HISTORY OF DEERPARK. 83

		Years.
Daughter Hannah	about	50
Daughter Margaret	"	80
Her husband, John Wallace	"	80

HEADS OF FAMILIES.

The ages of the following heads of families of this neighborhood, contemporary with the second generation, were as follows, to wit:

		Years.
Jacob R. De Witt	about	60
His wife, Jane Depuy	"	80
James Davis	"	80
His wife, Elizabeth Kater	"	70
William Geegge	"	80
His wife, Leah Davis	"	80

SLAVES.

The ages of the following slaves who were in this neighborhood, contemporary with the second generation, were as follows, to wit:

		Years.
Capt. De Witt's slaves:		
Cuffee	about	100
Frances	"	70
Woman	"	60
Esq. Depuy's:		
Man Peter	about	80
Woman Dinah	"	75
Capt. Cuddeback's:		
Woman Susanna	"	80

		Years.
Ezekiel Gumaer's :		
Man Jack	"	80
Esq. Van Inwegen's :		
Woman Susanna	"	70
James Swartwout's :		
Man Anthony	"	70
Woman Jude	"	70

The first two generations of the four ancient families had the small-pox naturally, without vaccination or dieting and without the attendance of a physician, and generally had it light. A few individuals, it was said, had only light symptoms of the disease and few pox ; yet certain individuals of two families had them hard. A few of the oldest of Depuy's family were considerably pock-marked, and a few of the oldest of Van Inwegen's family. The Cuddebacks and Gumaers were not pock-marked, and the Swartwouts very trifling.

There was in this neighborhood a contagious fever between the years 1750 and 1760, which was here termed "the long fever." It commenced in one of the summers near the end of harvest time, and was more mortal to the black people than the whites. Depuy lost several slaves, who died of this fever. He said the cause had been attributed to eating too many pigeons.

The second generation of the four ancient families, with few exceptions, remained healthy. Rheumatism sometimes afflicted the members of the second Gumaer family, but still were able to perform much labor and were strong, though not equal in strength to the Swartwout or Cuddeback families. All were men of six feet stature, excepting two of the Gumaer and one of the Van Inwegen family, and averaging near 200 lbs. weight.

LOWER NEIGHBORHOOD.

The following are the ages of the first generation of descendants of this neighborhood who were contemporary with the second of the other, viz.:

	Years.
Wilhelmus Cole died 1829, aged	88
His wife, Leah, died 1820, aged	77
Peter Kuykendal........about	80
Martinus (Martin) Decker died in 1802, aged	69
Simon Westfall died in 1805, aged	87
His wife	85
(Sally), wife of his son Simon, died 1837, aged	95
Solomon Kuykendall, Esq. } Unknown.	
His wife, Sarah Cole............ }	
Daniel Van Auken........aged about	80
His wife, Leah........ " "	80
James Van Fliet........ " "	80
His wife, Margaret Schoonover........ " "	80
Anthony Van Etten, Esq........ " "	—
His wife, Hannah Decker........ " "	85
Major John Decker........ " "	70
His wife, Sarah Hornbeck........ " "	80
Johannis (John) Decker........ " "	65
His wife, Deborah Van Fliet........ " "	50

			Years.
Capt. Johannis (John) Westbrook.....	"	"	80
His wife, Magdalena...............	"	"	75

POPULATION OF THE NEIGHBORHOOD OF PEENPACK.

MANNER OF LIVING, ETC., DURING THE REVOLUTIONARY WAR, AND FOR SOME YEARS THEREAFTER.

The second generation came on the stage of action and were married and had their farms granted to them in the intervening time between the French and Revolutionary wars, and commenced their business transactions when this part of our country was in a more thriving condition than it ever had been, in consequence of the circulation of a paper currency, which had become plentiful, and farmers made money faster than at any previous time ; but when the scale turned by its depreciation, its previous value was lost, which, together with the destruction the enemy made in the war, greatly reduced the property of the inhabitants.

In 1777, three forts were built in this neighborhood : one at the house of Esq. Depuy was vacated the 13th October, 1778, on which day the enemy invaded this neighborhood and burned this house, fort and other buildings of Depuy, in consequence of which all the inhabitants of this neighborhood were collected in the fort at Gumaer's and in Fort De Witt, to wit :

At Gumaer's the following families :

Whole No.

Philip Swartwout's, Esquire, which, after the
   death of himself and two oldest sons by the

	Whole No.
enemy, consisting of his step-mother, his widow, three sons, a son's wife and daughter, two slaves and an insane man...	10
Capt. Abraham Cuddeback's, which consisted of himself and wife, four sons, two daughters, a nephew and brother, and three slaves	13
Harmanus Van Inwegen's, Esq., consisted of himself and wife, seven sons, two daughters, a brother and five slaves............	17
Benjamin Cuddeback's were himself and wife, four sons, two daughters, a brother and two slaves........................	11
Jacob D. Gumaer's was himself and wife, two sons, five daughters and two slaves........	11
Peter Gumaer's, himself and wife, two sons and one slave....................	5
Ezekiel Gumaer's, his father, himself and wife, a son and one other boy and one slave....	6
Thomas White and wife...................	2
Mathew Terwilliger's, himself, wife, six sons and three daughters................	11
John Wallace's, himself, wife, one son and one daughter.....................	4
Average number of soldiers during nine months in each year, about.............	8
	—
	12
	23
	63
	—
Amount........................	98

	Whole No.
Benjamin Depuy, Esq.'s, family were in this fort about one year. It consisted of himself, wife, three sons, three daughters and seven slaves..................................	15
Whole number that year..............	113
At Fort De Witt were the following families: Capt. Jacob R. De Witt's, which were himself, wife, three sons, six daughters and four slaves.......................................	15
Moses Depuy's, himself, wife, two sons and two slaves...............................	6
Whole number......................	21
Samuel Depuy's, himself, wife, two sons and one slave..................................	5
Elias Gumaer's, himself, wife, four sons, two daughters and two slaves................	10
Abraham Cuddeback's, himself, wife, four sons and one slave.......................	7
Average number of nine month's soldiers about...................................	12
Jonathan Pierce's family and a few other individuals may have been in this fort 10 in number................................	10
	44
	21
Amount................................	65

	Whole No.
Esq. Depuy's family were in this fort during a part of the year, 15 in number..........	15
Whole number...................	80

There were some children born in both forts, which are not included.

LOWER NEIGHBORHOOD.

ITS FORTS AND SOME OF ITS WAR OCCURRENCES, ETC.

Previous to the invasion of this neighborhood by the Indians, three forts had been built in it in 1777 or '78 ; one at the house of Major Decker, where George Cuddeback now lives*, one at the house of Daniel Van Auken, near the present brick house of James D. Swartwout, Esq. †, and the other at the house of Peter Decker, in the present village of Port Jervis. The fort at Major Decker's was convenient for the families of Esq. Anthony Van Etten, Sylvester Cortright, Capt. Westbrook, Moses Cortright, Abraham Van Auken, and Schoonhover ; and the fort at Van Auken's was convenient for the families of James Van Fliet, Solomon Kuykendall, Esq., Simon Westfall, John Decker, and one or two other families ; and the fort at Decker's ‡ was convenient for the families of Wilhelmus Cole, Martinus (Martin) Decker, Samuel Caskey, James Davis and Utley Westbrook.

---

* Now (1889) occupied by Henry G. Cuddeback.

† Now (1889) owned by Ludwig Laux.

‡ Located upon the present site of the old stone house in Germantown, formerly occupied by Stephen St. John, deceased, and his family.

HISTORY OF DEERPARK.

On the 20th of July, 1779, Brant, with a corps of Indians and tories, invaded this neighborhood. The occurrences of which and of the battle of Minisink, one or two days afterwards, are contained in Eager's History of Orange County, page 388, &c., relative to the invasion and in relation to the battle see page 490, &c. There were about 18 families in this neighborhood who suffered in a greater or less degree the effects of the war, and a great proportion of them lost much property by the plunder and destruction which the enemy made by taking some of the best horses, plundering houses of goods and wearing apparel, burning of houses, barns and other buildings. In addition to which a few prisoners were taken, two of whom were slaves and two or more were killed. This invasion caused many of the best citizens of Goshen and vicinity to volunteer and pursue the enemy. The result of this was a more grievous calamity than the former, the results of which can be obtained as mentioned.

The number of children and domestics of each family in the lower neighborhood I cannot correctly determine, but contemplate the number of children to have been nearly as follows, to wit:

Anthony Van Etten......................	15
Daniel Van Auken......................	15
Major John Decker......................	6
Moses Cortright.................about	7
Jacob Schoonhover................about	3
Abraham Van Auken................. "	4
Capt. John Westbrook............. "	7
John Decker, Sr..................... "	6
Sylvester Cortright................. "	4

HISTORY OF DEERPARK. 91

—— Decker........................	"	4
James Van Fliet...................	"	8
Solomon Kuykendall...............		None.
Simon Westfall....................	"	6
Wilhelmus Cole....................	"	4
Peter Kuykendall..................	"	5
Samuel Caskey....................	"	6
Martinus (Martin) Decker..........		3
Utley Westbrook...................		2
Whole number....................		105

The number of children of those 18 families, according to my recollections, cannot have been less than 100, and may have been as many as 110. How many of them grew up to years of maturity, or how many died previous thereto I do not know. Major Decker had two or three children by his first wife, who died young; and John Decker, Sr., had one or more by his first wife, who also died young before the war commenced, but all of them after the decease of their respective mothers. The loss of a mother will affect the feelings of some children much, and no doubt many a child dies in consequence of the melancholy state of mind produced by such a bereavement. There were two or more premature deaths of boys or young men, and there may have been a few natural deaths in this neighborhood of which I have no recollection.

PEENPACK NEIGHBORHOOD.

The following were the number of children of each family in it during the war, and of two contemporary families who came into it after the war ended, to wit:

Children of	Esq. Swartwout:	4
"	Capt. Cuddeback	6
"	Esq. Van Inwegen	10
"	B. Cuddeback	6
"	J. D. Gumaer	7
"	P. Gumaer	4
"	Ez. Gumaer	2
"	J. Wallace	2
"	M. Terwilliger	9
"	Esq. Depuy	6
"	Capt. De Witt	9
"	M. Depuy	3
"	S. Depuy	3
"	Eb. Gumaer	6
"	Ab. Cuddeback	4
"	Widow Cuddeback	3
		84
Residents after the war ended.	{ J. Davis	7
	{ W. Geegge	2
		93

Of these 93 children a son of Ezekiel Gumaer died at the age of nearly five years, a daughter of Benjamin Cuddeback at the age of about six years, and a son of Esq. Van Etten, aged about 12 years. A son of Benjamin Cuddeback (Levi), died prematurely after he became a man, of a colic, caused by eating too many wintergreen berries, and a son of Abraham Cuddeback, Sr. (Philip), also died prematurely after he had arrived at manhood, of consumption, caused by overheating himself to put out a fire in the woods. Both these occurred a few years after the war ended. All the others lived until after they were married and had families of their own ; but the greatest part of them did not become as old as their respective parents. The first wife of James Swartwout died in the fort at Gumaer's, of consumption, within about one year after she came into it, aged about 25 years ; and Peter Gumaer died of palsy in this fort, near the end of the war, aged 71 years. There also were five premature deaths caused by the enemy—that of the three Swartwouts in this neighborhood, as has been mentioned—Gerardus Van Inwegen at Fort Montgomery, and Mathew Terwilliger, in the Minisink battle.

The following exhibits a certain number of the children mentioned who became as old, and older, than their respective fathers and of those who did not attain to such an age. In this I have excluded those families I could not ascertain, in consequence of having removed into other parts of our country, and of those untimely deaths not ended by nature's process, which leaves for calculation the following families. The left hand column of figures shows the number of those who became as old, and older, than their respective fathers, and the right hand column the number of those who did not arrive to that age, to wit :

Parents.	Oldest Children.	Youngest Children.
Capt. Cuddeback	2	4
Esq. Van Inwegen	2	8
Benj. Cuddeback	4	2
J. D. Gumaer	0	7

Parents.	Oldest Children.	Youngest Children.
Peter Gumaer...............	0	4
Ez. Gumaer.................	1	2
Esq. Depuy.................	4	4
S. Depuy...................		3
Eb. Gumaer.................	0	6
J. Davis...................	1	6
Wm. Geeggc.................		2
J. R. De Witt..............	4	5
	18	52

This calculation, being as near as I can ascertain the same, in respect of correctness, shows that only about one-quarter of the children of those families became as old as their respective fathers.

This great degeneracy will naturally lead to an inquiry respecting the cause of the same. To answer which, or to throw some light on the subject in relation thereto, I consider it necessary to state the manner and circumstances of life of each generation, as near as I am able to do it, to wit:

THE FIRST GENERATION

Being the children of the first pioneers, who settled in Peenpack at a time when there was was no other production in this part of the country for them to live on than the meat they could obtain of the wild animals, fowls and fishes before they raised grain or other productions for their diet, and we have reason to infer that after raising grain they only pounded it fine to answer for meat soups and such bread or cakes as they could make of it, to eat with those meats, and that these were their chief or only eatables for some years before they became enabled to have any other diet. They may, in the first instance, have obtained some meal from Rochester or vicinity, but after raising enough for their use it is probable they would rather use it pounded than to take it to the nearest mill, at that time, to get it ground, in which latter case the bran remained in the meal and as they could obtain good pounding stones and blocks from the Indians to pound their grain, and as the bran in grinding as well as pounding would remain in the meal, and as the nearest mill must have been about 25 or 30 miles from their neighborhood, we have reason to believe that they pounded their grain for soups and bread before mills were erected in this town ; and that the greatest difference between the diet of those families and that of the Indians, was that the former ate a greater proportion of vegetable productions than the latter. The men of this generation of descendants were generally stronger than those who succeeded them, from which it appears their eatables were healthful and that their drink, which was the best of spring water, also promoted health, and that all other circumstances which attended them were also of a healthful character, to wit : a pure air of the atmosphere, not impregnated with the exhalations from bad, stagnant waters ; brooks and small streams of clear water running down the mountains into the Neversink, creating a river of clear water passing through this valley ; such log houses as would let the fresh air of the atmosphere pass freely into them towards the large fire they kept up in cold weather, and their continual exercises in their boyhood with the Indian children in hunting, fishing, &c., and in all their sportive exercises of running, wrestling, &c., all had a tendency to promote health and strength and fit them for the labor they had to perform as they advanced in growth and after arriving to manhood, in respect to which however some parents were more indulgent than others, and those of the most persevering business character compelled their children to labor harder than those parents who were less persevering.

SECOND GENERATION.

My own recollection reaches no further back than the time in which all of them had families and when most of their children were small, but I have understood that their bread was made of unbolted wheat meal sifted through hand sieves to take out the coarse bran, until after they had grown up to years of maturity, and that after bolting meal was first introduced some persons said it was too extravagent to use only the fine flour to eat and to use all the rest for feed. During this time, and until all had families, many deers, bears, raccoons, wild fowls and fishes continued to exist, and the inhabitants were furnished with many meats, in consequence of which they did not make use of as much pork and beef as they did after those wild creatures and fishes became scarce.

As far back as I remember, being from about the year 1774, in my father's family mush made of Indian meal and milk (generally buttermilk), bread and milk, buttermilk pop of two kinds and bread and butter was a very general diet, not only of his family but of all those in the forts during the war and for some years thereafter throughout this neighborhood. It was also very common to have a dinner pot of pork and beef, or either of these boiled together with peeled potatoes, turnips or other sauce. The bread used during this time was rye bread, not as white as we generally now have it. It was very common to have a pot of sweet milk thickened with wheat flour lumps boiled every Sunday morning for breakfast and for a part of the dinner. These were the most general diet during the warm season of the year. In winter, a greater proportion of meat, potatoes, turnips and other vegetables, dried apples, pumpkins, beans, &c. were eaten, and less milk diet; yet the supper generally consisted both summer and winter of mush and milk or buttermilk pop, except in families during a time where cows happened to be all dry. The supper was had without any addition except in the long summer days when bread and butter was added. Some buckwheat pancake was generally eaten in winter. Now, in addition to those common diets, they sometimes had as a rarity, wheat flour shortcakes, doughnuts boiled in hog's lard, pancakes baked thin in a frying pan, puddings and dumplings boiled in water and eaten with a palatable gravy, chicken pot-pie, chicken soup, eggs boiled or fried and sometimes used in other different ways; many apple pies and huckleberry pies were made when these fruits and berries were plenty. They also had for winter rarity sausages of hog's meat, &c.

In respect to the other attendants of air, water and

exercise which have heretofore been mentioned, this generation enjoyed all these in the same manner as the first, but these had superior dwellings which were comfortable stone houses which every farmer, with very few exceptions, in this town possessed before the Revolutionary War commenced. These were closer than the first dwellings erected here, but still not very tight houses. Each room generally had an outside door, and all the rooms generally were on the lower floor; the chamber above these was used for granaries, flour barrels, and to store many different articles. The cellars were used for their milk and dairy articles, meat casks, cider barrels, winter apples, potatoes, turnips, and other vegetables. These cellar articles were not saleable in former times, but were generally used by the families who produced them.

The table furniture generally consisted of ordinary table knives and forks, pewter plates, pewter basins and platters of different sizes, pewter spoons, and a pewter mug which would contain about two quarts of cider, on which was a cover to open and close by means of a hinge, which last article was generally brought on the table for drink when the meal consisted of meat and hearty victuals, but was not used with their milk diets.

In the time of the war many of those articles were destroyed, and wooden plates, wooden bowls and dishes of different sizes were manufactured with a turning lathe and used for table furniture.

Now, although our parents lived in this plain and simple style, yet our mothers were as neat and clean housekeepers as their circumstances and business concerns would admit. They generally cleaned house every spring and fall, in which they scrubbed and washed with soap-suds the under part of the upper floor and beams, and whitewashed the walls, and every Saturday scrubbed and wiped the floors of their sitting rooms and kitchens. Floor carpets were not used in their time. The linen shirts, trowsers and frocks of the men and boys, and the linen clothes of the women worn during one week, were in the next boiled in a pot or kettle of lye, and, after a proper time, the pot was carried out to a pounding block, where, while hot, the clothes were taken out by pieces and battled on the block with a battle, and then put in a tub of soap-suds, made of soft home-made soap, in which the same was washed and thereafter rinsed in clean water and dried. Our fathers, their sons and slaves, labored hard in the hot season of the year and often wet their shirts and trowsers with the sweat of their bodies, and this manner of boiling, battling and washing those linen clothes was very effectual to clean the same.

All the travel before the war, in time of the war and for some years thereafter, was performed on foot, on horseback, and in lumber wagons and lumber sleds. In this manner people visited each other, and attended to all their religious and other meetings, and to all their traveling business concerns. Many of the women had become habituated to ride on horseback, and had their side-saddles for the same. When a dance was had, the young men fetched the girls on horseback, and the young man's horse became the carrier of him and his lady, who mounted on it behind him. In those times no paints adorned the houses of our fathers, nor articles of fancy their rooms. No fanciful tables or table furniture; no great variety of eatables and drinks were furnished for one meal; no clothing of superfine cloth or silk was worn in those times, nor even a pair of boots and rarely a fur hat. Pleasure wagons and pleasure sleighs did not ease and make comfortable the travels of our parents; no umbrellas covered their heads from the rays of the sun and the storms through which they had to pass. All of which articles are now furnished in great abundance, and generally all can enjoy more or less of them.

The buildings of those times, especially before the war, for storing grain, hay, horses and cattle, consisted of a barn and one or two barracks for each farmer, all covered with straw roofs. The barns were built nearly square on the ground, with a floor through its middle and a stable along one side for horses and one along the other side for cattle. When the barn would not contain all the grain raised on the farm, one or two barracks were erected by setting four or five long posts in the ground, hewed eight square, tapered towards the top end. Holes to contain iron bolts about an inch and a half thick were bored through each post at about one foot and a half apart, from the bottom to the top. These holes contained the bolts on which the frame of the roof laid, which was raised to the top of the poles by means of a windlass, and, after being filled with grain, whenever any of it was taken out, the roof was let down therewith to prevent rain and snow from blowing on it.

This generation generally ended their days after the commencement of a great change in our country; and by contrasting their manner of life with that of the present time (now 1858), we behold the great change made in a term of about half a century in the habits of life in this town.

THIRD GENERATION.

Between the years 1780 and 1800 this generation of the Peenpack neighborhood, of which I am a member, and the second generation of the lower neighborhood, came on the stage of action and commenced their own business transactions, in which we generally followed in the habits of our parents in respect to labor and diet, which continued for some time after the war ended. A change from the moral behavior of our parents was generated among the young people in the time of the war, and rude, vulgar and uncivilized habits had been acquired. After the war ended West India and York rum was introduced into this part of our country after stores became established in it, and farmers generally began to use these liquors in time of harvest and haying, during which time, in the first instance, a dram was taken early in the morning and work commenced and continued until about 8 o'clock, when breakfast was taken and then a bottle which held near a quart was filled with liquor and taken to the field for about six laborers, to last that day. This had been a practice before the war commenced and was considered to be an antidote against people injuring themselves by drinking cold water when the body was much heated by labor ; and as those liquors enlivened people and made them more vigorous to perform work during their operation, it was thought to be profitable in that respect. These, and the use of cider, were the first changes in this town, from the habits of the people in the time of the war.

USE OF SPIRITS AT FUNERALS AND WEDDINGS.

Liquor was used at funerals. The practice was to give each person a dram before entering the house in which the corpse was. This was done by two men who were placed with liquor at each door of the house or each side of one door, and was thought in those times to be an antidote against contagion, and for that purpose a dram was given to each bearer before he performed his official duty. Rum and cider were also used to treat people for their services in assisting in raising buildings after the war had ended. Rum was also used at weddings to treat the friends who attended it. In those anterior times and even within my own recollection, it was customary to invite to a wedding all the young people in this present town and some down the Delaware in New Jersey and Pennsylvania; and people, after the war ended, had not the means to furnish a variety of good victuals for their friends and neighbors who, yet treated them with those liquors, which had a superior estimation in those times to that of the present. They cheered and made lively and sociable the friends and neighbors who collected together, with trifling, if any, evil consequences, for people in those days guarded themselves against drinking so much as to become intoxicated and I have never known of any farmer of the second generation becoming drunk, yet there may have been such instances, and in progress of years it became a custom to make many afternoon frolics with liquor to get different jobs of work done. This led to intemperance and their multiplicity was unprofitable in a neighborhood. The young people sometimes had rude dancing frolics, where their only beverage was rum which was used in different ways, clear, sweetened with sugar, or made into sling, milk punch, eggnog, &c. The quantity of liquor drinked at these frolics, and the rudeness of the times caused many a fist fight, and this fighting became common at other gatherings of people where liquor was drank.

The use of those liquors increased and others were introduced, such as gin, brandy and different sorts of wines, &c. All these, generally of foreign manufacture, in progress of time, were kept for sale in stores by the large measure, and in taverns by small measure, where travelers and others who entered the taverns could not only have a choice of the variety of liquors, but also have their palatable taste improved by the infusion of sugar and other articles, whereby slings, milk punch, eggnog, hot toddy and other palatable compositions were made and much drinked in taverns. And in process of time distilleries were numerously erected in this part of our country, and cider and rye whisky, peach brandy, &c. were distilled in great quantities and other liquors were sometimes formed out of these. All of this flooded our country with a great amount of liquors of different kinds, the use of which became so fashionable that the greater part of families generally kept some in their houses to treat therewith the friends and neighbors who should visit them, and occasionally to use it in the family.

After some years' continuance of this extravagant use of spirituous liquors, its pernicious effects became apparent, and the writings of those who exclaimed against it, the warnings from the pulpit, and at last the formation of temperance societies had the effect of making the practice of keeping and using liquor in families unfashionable, and it became generally abandoned and many refrained from its use. This was a fortunate change, for all classes of people had become sufferers from the bad effects of those habits which had principally originated from the introduction of the fashion of treating each other with those liquors prepared in the most palatable manner, both at home and in taverns ; and I have no doubt that more than one-half of the liquor drank in those days was merely to follow the fashion of the times. Men generally dislike to be different from others. This is a powerful inducement to sway men to conform in a greater or less degree to the customs and fashions of their time, and, when these happen to be pernicious, thousands sometimes become the sufferers from their evil consequences.

TREATING VISITORS.

About the year 1800, the practice of keeping spirituous liquors and other appendages in families to treat visitors commenced. In 1813, when I commenced housekeeping, I thought it necessary to keep liquor, sugar, &c., in the house to treat visitors, and from that time until temperance societies were formed, I thought I could not agreeably entertain a visitor without having those articles, and if I happened to have none in the house at such time I generally sent out for them.

Cider had been a very plentiful and common drink in this neighborhood for many years. Cuddeback and Gumaer had been in the habit of drinking wine in their country, and after settling here, it appears, made early provision to have cider for their drink; for there were apple trees in their orchards and in Van Inwegen's orchard between two and three feet in diameter in the time of the Revolution; and when Gumaer (my grandfather) built his house, before the French war commenced, he had an opening left in the back wall of his cider cellar for a gutter to pass through it from his cider press back of the house into the cellar, and this gutter and others led the cider into the different cider barrels in it. From which it appears that the making of cider had become quite a business at that time, and, as it was no salable article, it was generally all drank by the family and visitors and by the Indians. It was a common drink from the time it was made in the fall until spring, when Gumaer made beer to drink in warm weather, for which he had a large brass kettle set on mason work, a long building and other fixtures to make and dry his malt. The use of cider by the white people never made them drunk, but some Indians, if they could get enough to drink, would sometimes get both drunk and abusive, in consequence of which it was generally withheld from them after they had drank enough. In respect to which I will here relate an occurrence. A large, stout

Indian at a certain time, came to Gumaer's and asked for a drink of cider. The pewter mug, which held two quarts, was filled and given to him. He drank and set it down by him, which, after drinking a few times, he emptied and asked for more. Gumaer told him he had drank enough, and that he would not let him have more. The Indian, after asking a few times and seeing he would not get more, took the mug and went off with it. Gumaer went to the barn, where his black man, Jack (who feared no Indian), was threshing with other hands, and told him that the Indian had gone off with the mug and that he must go and get it from him. Jack went, overtook the Indian, got hold of the mug, and, after a hard scuffle, got it from him and returned to his work. The Indian also returned and followed Jack to the barn and challenged him to fight. Jack, having felt his strength, did not like to undertake it; but, after some provocation of the Indian, a severe, long and hard fight was had, in which Jack became the conqueror. He had had many a fist fight with the Indians, but said this was the hardest he ever had. The Indians, when they became somewhat intoxicated, would often fight each other, in which they would make great exertions to get hold of each other's heads and try to twist each other's necks. From all of which, it appears, they could drink more cider than the white people and enough to make them drunk, against which the latter had to guard to evade the trouble of their intoxication. They would never revenge injuries which emanated therefrom, but imputed the same to the liquor as the sole cause.

After rum was kept in taverns in our neighborhoods

a company of Indians from other places sometimes came here to have a drinking frolic, for which they procured rum and selected a place for that purpose at a distance from the dwellings of the white inhabitants, so as not to disturb them, where they appointed two of their number to keep sober to watch and prevent them from hurting each other. To these two men they gave up all their guns, hatchets and knives, who hid them out of the way so that they should not have weapons wherewith to hurt each other ; and when all their arrangements were made they began to drink and soon got into a very noisy, turbulent and rude frolic, in which they would whoop, halloo, take hold of each other, scuffle, wrestle and sometimes fight. This they continued till their thirst for rum became satisfied, and after becoming sober, they were dull, stupid and deprived of the liveliness and activity they possessed before they commenced drinking, which had to be restored by abstinence.

NO DRUNKARDS AMONG THEM.

The first and second generations of the first four families who remained in this neighborhood had the free use of cider for a term of about one hundred years, including the time of the war, in which they could not have it, and during the greatest part of all that time had the means to procure as much other liquor as they craved, and yet not a single individual of them became a drunkard. When they came into company where rum or other spirituous liquors were drank, they would become lively, cheerful and humorous, by partaking of the same, but not as the saying is, "under foot." Such instances of sobriety, under such attending circumstances, for such a length of time, seldom occur.

We of the third generation, as well as our forefathers, have also been in a like habit of drinking cider during the greater part of our lives, and for many years in the habit of drinking all sorts of spirituous liquors without a single individual of us becoming what is termed a drunkard, but two or three of our class did sometimes become intoxicated and made a considerable approach towards being entirely overcome by the effect of liquor. Such also was the advancement of Gumaer toward those allurements as has been mentioned and there have been rare instances of some of us of sober lives becoming intoxicated. It is now (in 1858) 168 years since this neighborhood was first settled. Take 28 years from this time for the growth of an orchard to make cider, and 140 years remain for the use of its production which must have become plentiful within a less time than 28 years, for the first orchards of Cuddeback and Gumaer and one of Swartwout, which became Van Inwegen's, were on the very best of their river flats and must have had a very quick growth; the trees became large and were between two and three feet in diameter about the year 1780 when they appeared to have their full growth and some limbs began to die. From all of which we have reason to infer that the manufacturing of cider commenced here before the year 1720 and that much of it had been drank here from that time until the year 1840, previous to which its use began to abate and within that time many other spirituous liquors have been used with a mere trifle of intoxication for so long a time.

Now, although we and our forefathers received a mere trifle of the bad effects of liquors in this respect, yet the constitution of some of us must have been injured by their use. I, myself, have experienced the bad effects therefrom in respect to my own constitution, which at one time became so weak against its effects that if I drank so as to feel the least alteration from its influence it hurt me. This, however, was not the case with many others; some hard drinking men who came here among us remained healthy and lived to be old. Whether such would or would not have arrived to an older age without the use of liquor is uncertain.

Our diets continued to be the same as has been mentioned for some years after the Revolutionary War ended; but the diets of mush, &c., which were eaten with milk, began to be abandoned after different kinds of teas and coffee began to be used, and, after becoming generally used, the milk diets were in a manner wholly abandoned. In these drinks a little milk and sugar was put; molasses also was very plentifully used, and with this, sugar and other articles, many palatable, different kinds of sweet cakes, pies, &c., were made; also, different kinds of spices became fashionable for adding agreeable flavors to some diets. Now, all these are eatables and drinks which we did not have in our early days. In addition to all these we now have different kinds of preserves made with sugar, molasses, and different sorts of fruit, berries, &c., and some other diets we did not have.

After tea and coffee had been used for some time, they were preferred by the young people to the milk diet; but some of the older class, who had been habituated to eating buttermillk pop, mush and milk, and other diets, often chose to have these in preference to tea or coffee. Such are the effects of habit.

As to our industry and labors for the support of our families and to make advancement, they continued during our lives to be about the same on an average as those of our parents, in which some were more persevering and others less than their respective parents.

The inhabitants of the lower neighborhood who were contemporary with our parents, and those who were the same with ourselves, have also continued and progressed in about the same manner as we and our parents have done in the habits of life mentioned.

After our manner of living changed, we were from time to time afflicted with ailments and diseases which all have continued to suffer at times, more or less, until the present time ; but of late years have not had such mortal distempers in this vicinity as some we had at certain previous periods.

PHYSICAL STRENGTH OF FIRST GENERATION.

The first generation of the sons of the four families were reputed to have been strong men. It was said that the three eldest sons of Jacob Cuddeback, Benjamin, William and James, could carry 12 skipple wheat (9 bushels), by putting it into four three-skipple sacks, and, placing one under each arm and taking hold with each hand of the top of the others, could, on a barn floor, in this manner carry it from one end of the barn to the other; and that Anthony Swartwout's two sons, Samuel and James, could do the same, and that Harmanus Van Inwegen's son Gerardus, who was a smaller man, could carry it a few steps. Abraham Cuddeback, youngest son of his father, could not do it, nor Peter Gumaer's son Peter, so that only two out of eight were unable to carry it. From which the difference of their bodily strength, and that of those now on the stage of action becomes apparent.

The degeneracy of the inhabitants of this neighborhood has not been confined to them alone, but has extended from here down the Neversink and Delaware rivers throughout the Holland Dutch settlements; also from this neighborhood to Kingston. In the lower neighborhood in this town formerly were men as stout as those mentioned. It was said that one man in it could add one more bag of wheat and hold it with his teeth, and carry 15 skipple wheat (11¼ bushels).

Among the first generation along the Delaware river in the States of New Jersey and Pennsylvania, were men of equal strength with those mentioned, but not generally as strong. Such was also the case in respect to the inhabitants from here to Kingston.

The second generation of the four families did not arrive to as great bodily strength as the first, but still were strong men. All of them, excepting three, were men whose stature averaged about six feet, and their average weight was near 200 lbs. when in prime of life. Two of the three, who were of shorter stature, averaged about the same weight. I have seen the smallest, lightest and weakest man of their whole number with only the use of one hand, take a short three skipple sack, filled with rye, from the ground and put it on his shoulder. There were twelve of these men, and nine of them had families. These had 36 sons, who were all inferior in bodily strength to their respective fathers, and were all smaller and lighter men, excepting a few of the sons of Cornelius Van Inwegen, who were taller and may have been heavier than their fathers, and nearly or quite as strong. All the others were inferior to their fathers, and some much weaker in strength. Such a change in the bodily characteristics of these sons from that of their fathers must have proceeded from their different habits during the time of their respective growths, in which there was some difference, both in respect to diet and other attendants. The first (being the second generation) during their growth had for their eatables bread of unbolted wheat meal and meat soups, thickened with such meal, and they had a great proportion of wild meat of animals, fowls and fishes, which were yet plentiful here at that time. These diets their children did not have during the time of their growth, excepting a meal of fresh wild meat sometimes. They had rye bread and pork and beef, preserved with salt. This meat was generally used for dinner, together with some potatoes, turnips, and other kinds of roots and vegetables. Bread and butter, mush and milk, and other milk diets, potatoes, turnips, and other roots and vegetables, were plentiful here during the growth of the first as well as the second of those two classes of people. Now, in addition to the change mentioned, there was another of a different nature, which must have affected in a small degree the growth of the first, and in a great degree that of the latter. This was the effect of the French and Revolutionary wars, in each of which a fort was built at the house of Gumaer, and his neighbors all collected in it, which had the effect of creating more impure air in it than when occupied by one family. This, in the first war, could not hurt the constitutions of the children as much as in the next, because its duration was shorter, and most of them were sent from here to relatives in other places, and there were not as many in the fort as in the last war when the number in it of all classes was about 100 from the time the fort was built in 1777 until the war ended. The walls of the house, both in the rooms below and on the chamber, were all lined with beds, and although the inmates of the house remained healthy, yet the collection of so many people in it, and their beds and bedding, must have created much impure air, especially in the night when the doors were shut and all were in it, whereby the constitutions of the children must have become weakened and their growth retarded, so as to have remained both weaker and smaller than what they would have been if the war had not occurred. This stagnation of growth, which caused the third generation to remain inferior in strength to their respective fathers, did not continue to debilitate in the same ratio, the fourth class, but these arrived to about or nearly the same strength of body as that of their fathers. In relation to health, however, there has been a gradual decline, and people have now become more subject to disease in this town than in former times.

The Holland Dutch, who settled throughout this valley, must have had sound and strong constitutions, which their children inherited unimpaired, and the manner in which they were brought up and lived during the time of their growth in this valley must have been very conducive to sustain health and promote strength.

CHARACTERS.

There are certain predominating characteristics in families which, in some cases, will remain in their descendants from generation to generation for a great length of time, and some of those of the first pioneers have thus continued in some degree in their line of descent up to the present time ; and where intermarriages have occurred, of such different characters, they have generally become united in the children and, in some cases, this union resulted in better characters than that of either of the originals, and in others, worse.

In respect to the characteristics of five sons of the first families who remained in the Peenpack neighborhood, I will here give a short narration, to wit :

Major James Swartwout was a large, heavy, strong, portly and likely man, of a noble and dignified appearance, very suitable for a military officer, and was possessed of a spirit as noble as his appearance. He was very witty, jocose and humorous in conversation (these were Swartwout family traits), and he was too liberal and easy in his business affairs to accumulate property, in consequence of which he became much involved. He was generally consulted in matters of difficulty, in respect to which I will relate one instance, to wit :

At a certain time after the fall of a light snow, the members of a certain family who were neighbors to him, discovered apparently the tracks of a person on the roof of the house where no person could walk, which extended from one end of the roof to the other end. This alarmed the family, who thought it ominous of some calamity which would happen to them, and after some conversation respecting it, concluded it was best to send for Major Swartwout, to see what he would think of it. They accordingly got him there, who, on viewing it, concluded in his mind that it had been done by some person, and mistrusted a slave of the family, who kept near them to hear what would be said respecting it. He stepped up to the black man and accused him of doing it, which was denied. The Major told him he had done it and that if he did not own it he would give him a flogging, and still denying, the Major took a gad and gave him two or three whippings before he would own it, and after owning it the Major told him if he would tell how he did it he would let him go. He said he took a long pole and fastened a shoe to the end and therewith made the tracks. This eased the family of their fearful apprehensions.

William Cuddeback was a man of somewhat over six feet stature, coarse-boned, muscular and lean. He was strong and very nimble, and could outrun many young men after he was fifty years old. In the French war, after his hair had begun to turn gray, he outran a soldier who thought himself swift. He was very talkative and witty, and I think from what information I have had in relation to him, that he never had his equal in this town for humorous discourse and a display of wit properly and suitably applied. He was characterised as a wise man in his time. Argument was his hobby, and, as there was much of it in his time in relation to the Scriptures, he, although uneducated, became so versed therein that when among strangers he was often thought to be a well read man. He was a disbeliever in the superstitious notions which many people in his time had in relation to witchcraft, &c., and would often tell very laughable occurrences in respect thereto. He was somewhat slack in his business concerns and careless in paying attention to the same, but he always had help enough to manage the business of his farm.

Peter Gumaer was a man of about five feet ten inches stature. During the time of my acquaintance with him he was fleshy and fat, and in his younger days was a very persevering business man. He never was a hard working nor an idle man himself, but all his children and slaves performed a great amount of labor. His family produced a greater amount of farmer's productions than any other farmer within 20 or 30 miles distance from his residence, and he had all the necessary fixtures for his different branches of business in the best manner of his time. He would not suffer idleness in his family, and was inimical to it in others. He was a man of good judgment and of an honest and independent principle.

Gerardus Van Inwegen was a man of about five feet eight or nine inches stature. He was lean, bony, muscular and strong, and had much of the Swartwout jocose and humorous disposition. He was the only son of his father, and was brought up without work, and in his neighborhood became fond of hunting, and did much of it in company with the white and Indian boys of the neighborhood, and in early life became a very skillful hunter and took great delight in it. He continued to follow it through life, and killed more deer, bears and other wild animals and wild fowls than any other man of his time in this vicinity, whereby he not only obtained a very plentiful supply of those meats for his own family, but contributed liberally to those of Cuddeback and Gumaer, his neighbors, and enjoyed a very happy life. He was much addicted to playing tricks on people, and, when any of them happened to be offensive, he could generally end the matter in good humor. (It appears those ancients generally were well calculated to extinguish those offensive occurrences and restore friendship, by means of which they maintained friendly relations with each other and with the Indians.)

At a certain time he put a mean, dirty trick on a company of squaws and their children, which they discovered in going to a certain place, and immediately laid it to Gerardus, and, on their return, stopped at his house and accused him of it. He asked what made them think he had done it. They told him no other man in the neighborhood would do such a nasty trick; that he was worse than a hog and they would have satisfaction for that trick. After some altercation respecting it, he got a pail of cider and gave them as much as they would drink, which cheered them all up and they went off in good humor, laughing at those who fared the worse.

Samuel Swartwout was reputed to have been a very

strong man, and naturally easy and very good natured, not easily provoked to anger nor easily scared. He, by hunting and trapping, obtained a supply of meat and some other necessaries for his family. He had a valuable farm, but had no help to work it. Laborers could not be hired. After Depuy married his daughter he brought some slaves from his father's, and, with these, Depuy worked the farm and produced much wheat and other grain. Swartwout was on very friendly terms with the Indians, and when he removed from the residence of his father, he settled, as has been mentioned, among a collection of Indians.

In order to give some idea of Swartwout's boldness and of having been so characterized, I will relate a certain transaction, to wit: A certain Indian in his time had made a false face of a very frightful appearance, which was obtained from him by two or three of the young men. It was said that when it was put before a man's face and a bear skin wrapped around his body, the appearance in the night was very terrifying. They gave the man so dressed the name of Santa Claus. On a certain winter evening this Santa Claus went round among the families and frightened the members of four of them by this imprudent exhibition. After this they concluded to try if they could not scare the fearless Swartwout. Santa Claus went and entered his house. Swartwout sat before the fire, and, on seeing him, rose from his chair, took hold of it, and put himself in a position to strike. Santa Claus, fearing the blow, said, " Uncle Samuel, don't strike." Swartwout told him to go out of the house, or he would split his brains, and added, " If you are the devil, or from the devil, go to where you belong."

These five men and their fathers had to encounter many difficulties to retain the possession of nearly half the land they claimed under the patent against Jersey claimants, and it appears they were well qualified in all respects to counteract them. An account of this is contained in Eager's history.

CHARACTERITTICS OF A FEW INDIVIDUALS OF THE SECOND GENERATION.

Capt. Abraham Cuddeback was a man of six feet stature and over 200 lbs. weight. He was strong and athletic, and could with ease jump a five-railed post or rail fence. He was very handsomely built, and in all respects a very good looking man. He possessed a great mechanical genius, dexterity and good judgment. When quite young, seeing how shoemakers and weavers performed their work, he commenced and did the shoe-making and weaving for his father's family, and became the best shoemaker and the best and quickest weaver before he was a man grown of any in this vicinity. In the time of the French war his father sent him to Old Paltz, where, and in Rochester, he followed weaving and had no equal in those places. After that war ended the people here generally were destitute of fanning mills, and cleaned their grain with hand fans. He had seen one at Gumaer's and may have seen a few at the Old Paltz. He undertook and made one for his father or himself, and afterwards made several; one for my father, which was done in a good and handsome workmanlike manner, with which was cleaned all the grain of those in the fort at my father's during the

Revolutionary War, and thereafter all his own grain during his life. Before the commencement of that war a Mr. John Williams had given him some instruction for laying out the frame work of a house and barn, from which he considered himself enabled to do the carpenter work of such buildings, and did the carpenter work of a house and one or two barns before the war commenced, and after it ended a house and barn for himself and two or three other barns. After the war ended, he made a turning bench, repaired the old spinning-wheels in the neighborhood, turned spools, clevises, &c., for rigging the same. Before the war commenced, the wagons here had all been obtained from Rochester, in Ulster county, some of which were nearly worn out at its end, and a few years thereafter he undertook to contrive how to make a wagon. He said the greatest puzzle he had in mechanical work was to study out rules to make the wheels (of which he was entirely ignorant), but, after thinking over it, he discovered by what means he could make the same. After this he made wagons in a good and workmanlike manner, and in as good style as those which had been obtained from Rochester. He afterwards made pleasure sleighs according to the Kingston fashion of his time, of which there were only one or two old ones in this neighborhood as good and handsome as those which, in his time, had been made at Kingston, except painting, which he did not do. He made the best ploughs, and all kinds of farming utensils, of any which were made in his time in this part of our country. He was the greatest marksman at shooting with a rifle and one of the best hunters. And, notwithstanding all these acquisitions and the attention he paid to his farm, he was one of the greatest idlers in the neighborhood, and did often for the sake of conversation visit his neighbors, and when in company of the best informed, would generally introduce subjects to create argument, either in accordance with his own views or contrary thereto, so as to produce argumentation in which he delighted and was the best means of discovering the natural and acquired abilities of his opponent. He said he knew the mental abilities and natural characteristics of nearly all the men who were contemporary with him for a distance of 20 miles down the Neversink and Delaware rivers, and 40 miles toward Kingston. In his time Marbletown was the general market place for the inhabitants in this valley throughout the distance mentioned, and their travel to and from market made a great intercourse of those people, whereby they acquired a general acquaintance with each other. In respect to which I will relate an occurrence. In the commencement of the Revolutionary War, John Westbrook, who lived about 20 miles distant from Cuddeback's residence, was elected captain of a company of militia, and, in saluting him, he was blinded by the discharge of one of the guns, and remained blind. About 15 years thereafter, Jacob Cuddeback, son of Capt. Cuddeback, went to Mr. Westbrook's, and, after speaking to him, asked Mr. Westbrook if he knew him. He said he did not, but the voice was that of Capt. Cuddeback, which he still remembered, and judged from the resemblance of the voice of the son to that of the father, though they had not been together during that time.

In addition to what has been said respecting his mechanical acquirements, he became a workman in the business of tailoring. In the commencement of the war there were no men tailors in this town, and he first cut for himself; in sewing his daughter assisted him, and thereafter sometimes cut for others; and in the winters, when all were collected in the fort, he and his daughter did so much at it, especially in cutting and making up of deerskin leather, that he became a good workman and had not his equal here before a Mr. Mather, a tailor by trade, came into the fort.

It was said that at a certain time he and his wife took each a pound of frolic flax to spin, which she refused to do for him. He said he would do it himself and beat her. She was one of the quickest spinsters in the neighborhood and thought that impossible, and one morning both commenced on a strife, and he did beat her. At the frolic they exhibited their yarn, and his was adjudged as good as hers. While spinning she lost a little time to suckle a child. If he had ever spun any it must have been when he was a boy. He had not his equal in this town cradling grain. It was said that a few others in their ordinary way of cutting might have been equal to him, but whenever he undertook to race with a man, he made a reserve that his competitor should cut as large a swath as himself and as good, which no one could do, and cut as fast as he could.

At a certain time in going with my compass and chain to take the distance across the Neversink river, to determine how long a bridge it would require to reach across it, at a place where it was contemplated to build it, I met Cuddeback, who asked me where I was going to survey. I told him to take the distance across the river, to ascertain how long a bridge it would require to reach across it. He asked me if that could be done. I told him I could do it. This appeared to be new to him and somewhat mysterious. A few days afterwards I saw him again, when he told me that he had discovered how the distance could be taken across the river, and informed me of the manner in which it could be done. He differed some from one of the theories by which it was sometimes done, but embraced the same principle and was as correct to ascertain the distance as that theory generally practiced where the land is level.

Having been commissioned captain of a company of militia at or before the commencement of the Revolutionary War, he had many duties to perform during the same in that official capacity ; for which, as well as a mechanic, he had very suitable abilities. He was bold, sagacious, prudent, and tenacious of his honor ; he also was humane to those in his power. The following were some of his military services, to wit :

He was first stationed at Fort Montgomery to command the men of his company, who from time to time had to take turns to serve as militia soldiers in that fort ; and, previous to the attack of the fort, on the day it was made, he was sent with a company across the river to prevent the enemy from loosening the chain which had been put across it. This chain ran through the centre of three successive logs, fastened round it to prevent it from sinking, and was put there to prevent the English ships from running up the river. On those logs the company crossed the river and watched at the end of the chain until sometime in the night after the fort had been taken, when, from some unknown cause, the men became frightened and ran. He followed them a short distance, but could not find any of them. He staid there till morning, and was alone to defend the premises. After daylight he took a distant view of the English shipping; had an invitation to come on board, with a promise of good usage. He went home.

At Cochecton, 40 miles distant through the woods from this neighborhood, some families continued to live, and for their own safety kept in friendship with the Indians as long as they dared. In the first instance when danger began to be apprehended of attacks from the enemy, the Committee of Safety sometimes sent Captain Cuddeback with a few men to Cochecton to procure what information he could relative to the Indians, to discover whether there was any danger here of being attacked by them. In these scouts he had to be cautious to evade as much as possible the sight of the Indians, and entered that place secretly in the night, where at one or two houses he made secret inquiry respecting the Indians, and in the same night left the place and returned back, and, in going and returning, tried to discover signs of Indians. After two or three such scouts the Indians made an attack, in 1777, on the family of a Mr. Sprague, and next year on the family of a Mr. Brooks, some of whom they killed and others were taken prisoners. These attacks made the Committee act with vigilance. Persons suspected of being inimical to their country's cause were apprehended and tried. One or more of those at Cochecton were complained of, whom the Captain, with a few men, fetched from that place. In one instance he had trouble to save his prisoner from the revengeful abuse of a Mr. Brooks, one of the family who had suffered from the enemy as mentioned. The prisoner, to reward the Captain for interfering in his favor, presented him with a very handsome powder-horn and bullet pouch. These were used by the Captain during the war and thereafter, together with one of the best of rifles.

When the enemy in 1778 invaded the Peenpack neighborhood, the Captain resided at the Gumaer fort and had the command of the men in it. In the first instance he ordered all the pitchforks in the barn to be brought into the fort to prevent its being scaled, and directed the women to put on the spare coats and hats in the house, and each of them to take a pitchfork or other stick and put it on her shoulder. After being so equipped to appear like soldiers, he paraded all the men and the women back of the house and fort in single file, and, after the enemy came in sight, he ordered the drum to be beaten and marched them to the front side of the fort, where they all passed into it in view of the enemy, after which he ordered all the women and children to go into the cellar. Anna Swartwout, a large, robust woman, widow of Major Swartwout, asked permission to stay with the men in the fort to assist them, which was granted. She took one of the pitchforks to help defend the scaling of the fort, in case it should be undertaken. The enemy passed round the east side in open file at a distance out of gunshot; a few guns, however, were fired, but ammunition was scarce and reserved for actual engagement; balls were run the same day. As the enemy passed to where the barn intervened between them and the fort, the Captain and Jacob D. Gumaer went into it to prevent its being set on fire by them. Some of the enemy in passing along the river came to a woman, who had fled, and told her to go and tell the women in the fort that hundreds of Indians would be there before night, and if they wanted to save themselves they must leave the fort. This being done made a great scare among them, and some made ready to go out of it. The Captain ordered them all to stay in it, to which they quietly submitted. After the enemy had passed towards Fort De Witt, a little smoke was seen to rise on the roof of Cornelius Van Inwegen's house, which was about 60 or 70 rods distant from the fort. The Captain and Thomas White went and extinguished the fire, which had just begun to burn. It was said by certain tories, who returned after the war ended, that the enemy had such a good feast of victuals and cider at this house that they concluded not to burn it. The fire must have originated from the act of a single individual, or the burning of the barn. At Fort De Witt the enemy took a station on a hill, in woods, within gunshot of the fort, and fired several volleys against the wall of the house and picket fort. After a few volleys were fired, Benjamin Cuddeback, a brother of the Captain, challenged the enemy to show themselves, and, although they were out of sight, he, with a long Esopus gun, heavily loaded, returned some shots, whereby they became about as much exposed to his firing as the inmates of the fort were to their firing. In returning they passed on the west of the other fort, where they tried to catch some of my father's horses, which his black man Jack happened to see, who stepped out of the fort and shot, which started both horses and the enemy so as to let the horses go. A fire was returned at Jack, and the Captain pulled him back into the fort. The enemy left, took some of the best horses, plundered and burnt houses and other buildings, and that day went out of the neighborhood.

In July, 1779, after the lower neighborhood had been invaded by the enemy, and a corps of militia from Goshen and its vicinity who had volunteered to pursue the enemy arrived in that neighborhood, Capt. Cuddeback and some others out of this town joined in the pursuit, in which the officers, after having proceeded to a distance from the neighborhood into the woods, began to have their consultations in respect to continuing or returning, also in respect to the best place to attack the enemy, in case of undertaking it. The opinions of Captain Tyler and Captain Cuddeback, who were acquainted with the path and woods, were had. Tyler proposed to make the attack where the enemy had to cross the Delaware river, and Cuddeback to make it in the night, where the enemy should lodge for their night's rest; there to fall on them unawares, drive them from their prisoners and plunder, recover these and return homeward with them in the night.

Very reasonable objections were made to both these plans by the superior officers; but, in case of attack, Tyler's plan was preferred by the officers generally, and was urged, as is well known, by very improper means.

In the battle, Cuddeback, with a dress of the color of the leaves, one of the best rifles and other equipments, and a very great marksman, was one of the most important fighting men of the corps, and remained on the fighting ground until after the retreat had commenced, and until he saw he had to run to save his life, when he ran a short distance to one side of the course (the mass of men ran) where he squat down, cocked his rifle and kept ready to shoot any Indian who should happen to look at him, where he remained undiscovered by those who passed him until a large Indian, came slowly walking and looking round, at last turned his face towards him when he shot and again ran, and in coming to steep rocks he slid down the same on his back ; and when he came to a good place to hide he again hid and laid down. Here he remained until dark, and from thence in the night started for home.

The militia soldiers, like the Indians, fought from behind trees, stumps, rocks, etc. John Wallace, one of Cuddeback's militia company, kept near his Captain at the different stations to which he was from time to time removed by his superior officers. At one of which Wallace received a slight wound, and in the flight made his escape but became separated from Cuddeback, and in returning home hunted through the woods and killed three deer. After Cuddeback had been home three days, Wallace unexpectedly arrived with three deer skins on his back, to the great joy of his wife and two children.

Cuddeback commended Col. Tusten very highly, and said he felt sorry for him when he was wounded ; that when the retreat commenced he was called to where the Col. and other wounded officers and men were collected in the safest place, and was solicited to try and stop the retreat, but that was impossible ; it had become too general. He had to leave them to their fate, or become a sufferer together with them, and made his escape as mentioned. The retreat was caused by a hideous shouting, yelling and firing of guns, which had been undertaken by the Indians as a last resort to put their opponents to flight ; and it happened to have the desired effect. Until this occurence, the men who suffered much in different ways from heat, warm clothing, want of water and wounds, wonderfully sustained themselves for militia soldiers against an enemy who had very great advantages in all respects.

Cuddeback, in his domestic concerns, had a great share of indulgence towards his family and domestics, but was uncommonly severe in reproof if any of his children happened to do an act of which he much disapproved, although these never were of a criminal nature. He had an uncommon gift to stigmatize and reprove a bad action.

Benjamin De Puy, Esquire, was a man of about six feet stature, not as bony, muscular and strong as the descendants of the first settlers. He was a persevering business man, but after he had been a few years in this neighborhood he became too fleshy and fat to perform any labor on his farm himself, but still paid a very strict attention to his farming business, the labor of which he managed to have done by his slaves, and sons after they became able to work. He became a Justice of the Peace here of the former county of Ulster, and served many years in that office before, in, and after the war. He also served many years as a Supervisor of the old town of Mamakating. In the commencement of the war he was one of the Committee of Safety. He was the greatest supporter of religious worship in the Mahackamack congregation. He was tender and humane to his wife, children and slaves, and provided a very plentiful living for all of them, in respect to diet and the necessities of life, even to excess. He had a strong memory and retained much of what had transpired throughout this valley from here to Kingston.

Depuy was a heavy load on a horse and had about as good luck as Alexander the Great had in obtaining a suitable riding horse for him. This great conqueror had one to carry him safely in his great battles and extensive conquests, and De Puy had one which carried hm safely for many years and on many bad roads until age rendered him unable to continue his services. The former built a city and named it Bucephala, after the name of his great war horse " Bucephalus," and the latter continued to feed and nourish his horse as long as it lived, and even sometimes with bread. I happened to come to his house at one time just after he had given his horse some bread. He then told me that this horse had never fallen with him in all his travels. He related to me that at a certain time he and some other gentlemen went on a very rough, stony road along Basha's Kill in great haste to arrive in time at a certain meeting ; that some of the horses did often stumble, and in one or two instances fell, and that his horse traveled over it without making a single blunder. All his travels on this horse must have amounted to some thousands of miles distance. About one half of his farm was between one and two miles distant from his house, and whenever his laborers worked on those lands he generally went to them on this horse once or twice a day. He had to go every year twice or oftener to Esopus, 50 miles distant, to perform his official duties and to many other places where his civil and church offices called him. The horse was strongly built for carrying, had a slow, easy pace, and was very kind. The continual exercise De Puy had on his horse and sometimes in the wagon and sleigh for doing his business at the mill, stores, blacksmith's, &c., had a tendency to keep him healthy, yet he had a few short, hard sicknessess, but continued to live to a good old age, and in the last part of his life sold the part of his farm which he had retained and was removed by his sons to the town of Owasco, where, and in that part of New York, all his sons and daughters, excepting two, had previously settled, and there his mortal life was ended.

Philip Swartwout was a large, strong man, upwards of six feet in stature, portly and likely. Captain Cuddeback, who had seen General Washington at Fort Montgomery, said he had never seen a man who resembled Washington as much as Esquire Swartwout; the features of his face, his eyes, forehead, size and form of his body, all he said, had a great resemblance to those of Washington.

Swartwout in his business transactions was very persevering and honest. In his public acts he was also honest and persevering to obtain the objects of justice between individuals, and also to promote the welfare of the public. He was a Justice of the Peace of the former county of Ulster before the Revolutionary War commenced, and in its commencement became one of the Committee of Safety. After the decease of his father, August 21st, 1756, he became heir to his estate, which consisted of a good farm, but was so much encumbered by the debts of his father, that he concluded to let the creditors take it. These were relatives of his, who resided at Rochester, in Ulster county. They advised Swartwout to take the farm and they would give him his own time to pay the debts, in consequence of which he obligated himself to pay the debts and took the farm. His oldest boys must have been about 10 or 12 years old at this time. He had one man slave and an insane man lived with him, who remained in the family during life. With this help he commenced to work the farm, and, after his son James became old enough to learn the blacksmith trade, he built a shop, got a blacksmith, who, together with James, pursued that business, and the father, with his other sons and slave, worked the farm and made money fast, so that he paid all his debts, and had money standing out at interest when the war commenced.

Swartwout, as well as Depuy, was a great supporter of religious worship, and paid a strict attention to the preaching of the gospel.

Anthony Van Etten, Esquire, was from Rochester or its vicinity, where he had received a good education for his time. His visage and bodily form and size were said to have resembled his youngest son Anthony Van Etten, who was a man of about 5 feet 10 inches stature, and about 160 lbs. weight. He was a blacksmith by trade and became married to Hannah Decker, daughter of Thomas Decker, in 1750, and obtained from him a piece of land, on which he built a house and shop, and entered into the business of his trade, and got an apprentice to assist him. He soon received a great amount of work from the farmers and made money fast. He built the stone house in which his son, Captain Henry Van Etten, formerly lived, and, as he became enabled, bought land and obtained the old Van Etten farm, which consisted of some of the best land in this town. He and Esq. Swartwout, who were contemporary, both commenced business with small means, and became the most thriving business men in this town. Van Etten became a Justice of the Peace of the old county of Orange at an early period of his residence in this town, in which he officiated to the end of his life in 1778. His widow survived him many years. She was a short, strong woman of a good constitution, an affectionate mother and agreeable neighbor, sociable and much addicted to humorous conversation, and often told funny occurrences of former times. *

Cornelius Van Inwegen was a man of about 5 feet 8 inches stature, and about 170 or 180 pounds weight. In his boyhood, after he was able to handle a gun, he

---

* Anthony Van Etten, was a son of Jacob Van Etten, and Antie Westbrook, who were married at Kingston, Ulster county, New York, April 22d, 1719, they both being residents of that county at the time. They had a large family and came with them to the Delaware valley about 1730, taking up a residence at Namenoch, opposite the island in the Delaware now so called, on the New Jersey side. Their oldest daughter, Magdelena, married Rev. Johan. Casp. Fryenmuth. From their sons are descended the various Van Etten families of Orange county, N. Y., Pike county, Pa., and Sussex county, N. J.

Anthony was born about 1726 at Napenoch, Ulster county, and baptized at Kingston Ref. D. Church, June 12, 1726, At the time of his marriage, August 3d, 1750, he resided at Namenoch, but thereafter with his wife located in what is now the town of Deerpark.

The baptismal records of the Maghachemech Church furnish the names of most of their large family of children as follows :

Thomas, bap. Sept. 8, 1751 ; Antie, bap. Jan. 14, 1753 ; Janneke, bap. April 28, 1754 ; Margarieta, bap. Feb. 13, 1756 ; Levi, bap. Feb. 12, 1758 ; Alida, bap. Aug. 19, 1759 ; Hendricus, bap. June 14, 1761 ; Blandina, bap. Sept. 4, 1763 ; Maria, bap. Nov. 11, 1765 ; Thomas, bap. Oct. 16, 1768 ; Jacob, 1774 ; Anthony, bap. Oct. 29, 1780.

Of their sons, Levi married Grannetje Westbrook, and from them are descended most of the families now in Deerpark. Anthony, Jr., married Jemmia Cuddeback, and located in central New York.   A. V. E., Jr.

became very fond of hunting, and he and Capt. Cuddeback, when boys, generally hunted together, and both became well skilled therein ; which the latter partially quit when he arrived to manhood, but Van Inwegen continued to follow it through life and killed more deer, bears, and other wild animals and wild fowls, than any other individual of this town ever did since he became a hunter. No family in the neighborhood enjoyed as plentiful a supply of the best of wild meats as his family, and, being liberal therewith, he often contributed some to my father's family and to Capt. Cuddeback's, who were his nearest neighbors. The numerous skins of deers which he acquired were valuable for himself and family, and for all his neighbors. In his time the men and boys all wore short leather breeches of deerskin, and some of the men had leather coats to put on in dry weather to perform rough and dirty work, and in the latter part of his life some individuals wore leather frocks in which to perform such work. Moccasins of deerskin leather were also much worn in winter. Deerskin leather was valuable for the inhabitants of this town in the time of the war, in consequence of the inconvenience of manufacturing cloth during that time. In those cheap times, when rye and corn were only four shillings a bushel, a good buckskin was allowed to be worth from twenty shillings to three dollars before dressed.

Now, these characters, which differed very widely, were all necessary for the general welfare of the community. The other inhabitants of the second generation, and their contemporaries in the lower neighborhood as well as those mentioned, were useful members of society, and each did more or less contribute towards the welfare of others. They were generally an industrious, honest, prudent and economizing people, who obtained their living by the sweat of their brow, and had to manage their business suitable to their circumstances and means of procuring a livelihood.

Men in a state of nature, like the wild animals, generally live on the spontaneous productions of the earth, and each has to procure its own food after the parent's help becomes unnecessary. The first settlers here were nearly in the same self-procuring situation, and only had a few manufactured implements in advance of the naked-handed Indians.

By the introduction of scientific knowledge men have become dependent on each other, and thereby enabled advantageously to cultivate the earth and provide for a very numerous population, and also create enjoyments far beyond what the unimproved races of mankind can realize. The numerous branches of mechanical and scientific works and occupations employ millions of people, who obtain a living thereby. Each of these produce materials and literary works whereby others become interested, all of which create an extensive social intercourse which reaches all the civilized and manufacturing nations of the earth; and, even in a small degree, some of the unimproved races of mankind.

All this beautiful order among men, for which they are formed, suitable in body and mind, if the same could be sustained without imposition and unerring conduct in all respects, might render man very happy, but destruction has been the fate of the ancient civilized nations who had, in a greater or less degree, become an improved and scientific people, and good reasons must have existed for producing this extinguishment.

In the year 1792, I was constable and collector of the old town of Mamakating, in Ulster county, which then extended from the old county line near the present dwelling house of Philip Swartwout, Esquire, and son, about 20 miles northeasterly, and from Shawangunk Kill northwesterly about forty-five miles to or beyond Cochecton, and included part of the present towns of Deerpark, Mount Hope, Mamakating, Forestburgh, Lumberland and Cochecton. The town was divided into two collector's districts, of which mine was the largest, and the amount of tax I had to collect was £15 0s. 6d., ($37.56).

The highest taxpayer on the list was Esquire Depuy, whose tax was seven shillings, ten pence, one farthing, and the whole number of persons taxed in my district, 45 miles long and part of it about 12 miles wide, was 182. From this neighborhood to Cochecton, (40 miles distant) there was only a foot path through the woods on which I traveled on foot and carried a knapsack, in consequence of the scarcity of horse feed and provisions along it. Rafting masts, spars, logs, and a few boards had previously commenced. The timber at that time was principally got from the sides of the mountains and hills bordering on the river, under great disadvantages, for want of teams and a road, until one was made with the State funds from the residence or grist mill of Captain William Rose to Cochecton, about the year 1803. After this the lumber business increased rapidly and became very great, whereby the inhabitants of this town became greatly benefitted, both by the market it made for their produce and the money some individuals made by that business. At the close of the war Orange County was very thinly settled, and most of the land unimproved.

Low as the taxes were in 1792, I found several unable to pay a few pence, and thereby lost about the amount of my fees.

GREAT CHANGES IN AGRICULTURE, MANUFACTURES, TRAVEL AND IMPROVEMENTS OF EVERY KIND.

We of the third generation of the first four families and our contemporaries in the lower neighborhood, have passed through a period of time in which greater improvements have been made in our country than ever has been made within such a space of time in any country. Its equal, probably, will never again occur ; yet we know not to what state of improvement men will arrive.

The arts and sciences have been stretched far beyond their former bounds, and gigantic and minor productions have been brought to view by the labor and ingenuity our countrymen have displayed, and great are the benefits mankind have derived from their labors.

Some rulers of nations and great generals of ancient times have been highly honored for acts of murder and plunder to aggrandize themselves, who, instead of rendering benefits, were a nuisance in the world. Not so with our scientific men. They crave not the loud applause of the multitude, but their general welfare and their labors have created benefits far beyond what we can calculate, and all are more or less benefitted from the results of their labors.

We have been spectators of the great changes mentioned and have seen the time when the red men were yet among us, and were often refreshed and cheered by their white neighbors with something to eat and a drink of cider; and the time, when they disappeared and a great revolution commenced, and the effects of the war it created, the restoration of peace and the times when the constitutions of the several States, and of the United States, were, from time to time, formed and become established, and the effects of the laws which have from time to time been passed under those constitutions, and the great benefits which have resulted therefrom; also the career of our first and greatest statesmen, who exerted their powers for the good of their country.

And here let us not forget that in the days of our boyhood we have seen the time in which the military forces of our country, under great sufferings and privations, nobly sustained their country's cause to obtain an independent government, and have been spectators of its achievement and the great results which have emanated therefrom; in respect to which I will here give a very faint view of what has transpired in relation to the improvements our countrymen have made during the time of our life's journey, to wit:

We have seen the time of the commencement of the printing of newspapers in this part of our country after the war ended, and the rapid increase and vast extent to which that important business has arrived, whereby every citizen with small means can now have information of the acts of our legislatures and more than he can read of what continually transpires both in our own and other countries.

We have seen the time when schools were in their infancy in this part of our country, their progress and the vast extent to which they became multiplied, even so that almost every citizen of this State, and generally of the other states, has the opportunity of having his children educated according to and even beyond his pecuniary means. We have seen the time when there was not a minister of the gospel, lawyer or physician, within 20 miles distance from our present town, and have seen the continual increase of those professional men until every town in our county had more or less of them, and the increase of education, so that it reached nearly all the citizens, few of whom do not acquire enough to read and write, and a very great proportion have reached the higher branches of learning, and become fitted for all the different business transactions of our country.

We have been spectators of the time when all transportation on the Hudson river was done in vessels, whose speed depended on the winds which impelled them, and of the time when the ingenuity of Fulton, with the help of Chancellor Livingston, produced a steamboat wherewith the Hudson river was navigated, and, when thereafter others from time to time were built, until all the navigable waters with such boats in our country were therewith navigated, and even the Atlantic Ocean crossed to and from England and other places, and the time when other machineries began to be impelled by steam power and their increase until thousands got into operation.

We have been travelers on the early rough and

stony roads in Orange County and have seen the first construction of turnpikes in our county, and the great improvement of our highways, and at last have beheld the gigantic works of canals and railroads, on which the value of millions of property is annually transported to and from all parts of our country, and thousands of people are continually enjoying the easy and speedy travel thereby furnished.

We have been co-operators with our respective parents in producing all the articles of food and raiment for our own subsistence, and when we wanted a few articles we could not make, such as salt, iron, &c., we had to travel to the store of Nathaniel Owen, 22 miles distant or to the store of Cornelius Wynkoop, 40 miles distant, to procure the same. After this the ingenuity of some of our citizens produced machinery for manufacturing all the cloth we wanted for our use with much less cost and labor than what we could formerly manufacture the same ; and these are now so abundantly transported into all parts of our country, that our little town of Deerpark now has more stores in it than the whole county of Orange had at the close of the Revolutionary War, and probably as many as there were in both the counties of Orange and Ulster. These goods, by an exchange of commodities for the same, can now be procured so much easier than formerly that our former apparatus for manufacturing flax, wool and cotton into cloth has become useless. And these stores now contain such a variety of articles, that as a certain man once said " Many necessaries unnecessary.

We have taken wheat, rye and corn to New Windsor and Newburgh when these were very small places and when Goshen was a very small village, and have passed through the time in which all the other villages in Orange County had their origin and growth and in which the whole country west of the valley in which we reside, has become numerously populated throughout its present settled parts, in which many handsome and magnificent villages and cities have been built and now adorn those parts which, in our early days, were a vast wilderness.

We have seen the time when news traveled from the printing presses to us on horseback, and when the same became conveyed in light one and two horse wagons, and in progressing, stage wagons and steam boats became the swiftest carrier of news, and after the meridian of our lives the swiftest traveler ever before known came into operation, in which news, passengers and different commodities were conveyed to and from distant parts of our country, and in the last part of our life's journey originated the wonderful discovery of giving instantaneous information of any matter or occurrence for any distance to which telegraph wires can be extended.

We have been farmers and inured to all the different kinds of labor thereunto appertaining. We have in early life ploughed with wooden ploughs, to which a wrought share and coulter were fastened, sowed all our grain by hand, harrowed the ground with square iron teeth harrows, cut all our grain with scythe and cradle, threshed all our grain with hand flails, mowed all our grass with scythes, and raked our hay together with hand rakes, and commenced tillage when the soil of our river lands was reduced to its lowest state of nutrition since the time their cultivation was first commenced. In progressing from the beginning of our business transactions, we became ploughers with patent ploughs, constructed of wood and iron castings, on which many improvements were, from time to time, made and have passed through the time of the introduction of different kinds of cultivators to cultivate ploughed ground, and of sowing machines, reaping machines, threshing machines of different kinds, and different kinds of horse power to impel the same, mowing machines to cut grass, and different kinds of horse rakes to gather hay, and different kinds of corn shellers, cutting benches, churning machines, &c., &c. We have observed a slow improvement of the lands in this town, which commenced about the year 1810, and progressed very slow at first, but increased in rapidity until the present time, 1858, and lands in this town now produce about double what they did in their lowest state of cultivation. We have seen the time when society here was in the lowest and most degraded state in which it has ever been in this valley, and have seen its rise and progress from that state to its present good and moral behavior.

Now all these works, which are of inestimable benefit, are only a small part of the discoveries and improvements made by our countrymen in our time of life. We do not claim to have stood alone as observers, not that other countries have been idlers in respect to inventions and improvements, but that all our contemporaries, both in our own and other countries, have passed through a period of time which has produced greater and more wonderful discoveries than that of any other like term of years.

Our travel on this great highway of research is yet

rapidly advancing, and to what extent men will arrive is best known to the Great Architect who fills the universe with his works.

In consequence of the improvements mentioned and the great prosperity of our country, we also became spectators of their results in our manner of living, and although we have comparatively with others remained in humble walks of life, yet we have made great strides from our early habits, which, in the days of our youth, were governed by destitution and want of means to expand and gratify our desires. The greatest complaint, however, in those anterior times, was the burden of labor which all had to endure with greater or less perseverance, much of which has now been done away with by means of machinery.

Some years after the war ended the inhabitants of this town began to make money, and were enabled to live in a different style from that of their former habits, and articles of fancy were introduced. The acquisition of these progressed slow at first but increased as people advanced in property and became enabled to procure the objects of their desires, and the different luxuries thus introduced among us have continued to become more numerous until the present time.

By contrasting the manner of living of our parents with that of the present time, we behold the vast change made in a term of about half a century. When our manner of living became changed diseases began to afflict us, and these, as well as our habits of life, have continued to increase, which, together with the great addition of our population, now generates diseases which give employment to the physicians who reside among us.

SCARCITY OF PHYSICIANS IN FORMER TIMES.

The services of men of their profession rarely reached this valley in former times. At Goshen was one or more regular physicians in the time of the war, and in the State of New Jersey, about 20 miles distant from this neighborhood, was another. The latter sometimes attended Peter Gumaer, my grandfather, who was stricken with palsy near the time the war commenced, and he and Doctor Sweezy, from Goshen, attended to heal the wounds which Cornelius Swartwout received when the Indians invaded this neighborhood.

In the latter part of the war, and for some years after it ended, there lived an old man by the name of Bennet, on the east side of Shawangunk mountain in the present town of Mount Hope, who in his youth had studied medicine, but abandoned it before he became qualified to practice. He, however, was sometimes called on to attend the sick. He was poor and kept no drugs or medicines, but when called on would go and see what the ailment of the sick person was, and then go out and collect such roots and herbs as he judged best to cure the disease, which he used according to the dictates of his judgment. After people in our neighborhood began to be afflicted with diseases, and when it was considered necessary to have the attendance of a physician, this Doctor Bennet was employed; and he generally was quite successful in his practice. He several times cured a young man of colic, to which he was subject. This he performed by giving him an emetic, and after it had operated he gave him a physic.

It appears that the constitutions of people become adapted to the climate in which they reside, and to such habits of life as they from generation to generation continue to pursue, and a change of these will affect persons more or less. This is evident from what is known in relation to the different races of mankind, some of whom live very different from others, and the exchange of some, whose food differs very widely, would be mortal to many of one or both of those races who should make the exchange.

Eight of us, all descendants of the four families, now all residents of the lower neighborhood, excepting myself, remain yet travelers on the last part of life's journey towards that change which all flesh has to undergo to answer the purposes of the Creator.

BIRDS, REPTILES AND ANIMALS.

Among all the changes mentioned, some of us have been spectators of nearly an extinction of birds in our valley and its vicinity, many different kinds of which formerly visited us in the spring of the year and continued with us during the summer and a part of the fall months. Their active flights from place to place and from tree to tree, and their musical voices of different sounds enlivened and cheered our lonely valley. These all had to be active to gratify their cravings of what was necessary to sustain life. Some wandered along streams of water to procure their food; some hovered high in the air of the atmosphere, from which they surveyed the lands and waters below them to discover the objects they craved for food, from which elevation the hawk would sometimes dart swiftly downward among a flock of birds and catch and make a prey of one of them, as well as of his objects on the ground. The fish-hawk hovered over the waters, the chicken-hawk over the landscapes to entrap their prey. The owl made his excursions in the night to seek his food, and each of the different tribes of birds possessed its own means of obtaining a living. Many of the worms and insects on the ground, and of those small insects which impregnated the air of the atmosphere, became a prey of birds.

Among the different tribes of birds which visited us were the following, to wit : Blackbirds of different kinds, crows, robins, swallows of different kinds, nightingales, snipe of different kinds, killdeers, cranes of different kinds, hawks of different kinds, owls of different kinds, turtle doves, whippoorwills, wrens of different kinds, bluebirds, partridges, quails, wood-peckers, eagles, snow birds, and a few other kinds.

The pleasing enjoyments of all species of birds are evidences of the goodness of their Creator ; and the adaptation of all kinds of living creatures whatever to their respective modes of life, are evidences of a pre-existing plan for the formation of each, and the manner in which each shall be furnished and receive whatever is necessary for its preservation during life.

Snakes have also become nearly extinguished in this valley within the last half century, previous to which there were yet some rattlesnakes, pilots, blacksnakes, sissing adders, gartersnakes, greensnakes, and milk-snakes, and toads and frogs are not as numerous now as in former times.

Now, although some of these reptiles may appear to us as unnecessary nuisances, yet they undoubtedly have answered certain good purposes in their sphere of being. A few persons of this neighborhood have suffered from the bites of poisonous snakes, but remedies were here known in former times which saved the lives of those who were bitten. Their number within my knowledge was six.

There was a singular occurrence in Rochester, in Ulster county, in former times, to wit: At an early period of the settlement of that place, a certain man in time of harvest in going with a wagon, with shelvings on it, to fetch a load of grain, and, passing near a rattlesnake in the grain field, stopped his team, and, with a fork which had a very long handle, wherewith as he stood in the wagon he reached the snake and began to tease it and soon saw that it began to swell, and being anxious to see to what size it would expand itself, he continued to tease it until its body became swollen to a very large size, when it made a spring and passed over wagon and shelvings without touching any of it and came down on the ground on the other side of the wagon, and, in passing over it, the man very narrowly escaped being bitten in his face by the snake as he stood in the wagon. Such an occurrence was a good warning against trying such experiments.

Another occurrence of anterior times will show the effect of hunger, in the last stage of life, of a certain hawk.

At a certain time when Gerardus Van Inwegen and Abraham Cuddeback were catching pigeons with a net, a hawk came and lit on a fence near them, and continued there watching the pigeons until they had made some hauls ; and all the ado they made to spring the net, run to it, kill and carry the pigeons, &c., did not scare the hawk so as to drive him from his place, but from his action appeared to want a pigeon. This caused Van Inwegen to try the following experiment te catch him. He took a pigeon in his hand and held it at arm's length before him towards the hawk, and walked slowly towards him, and when the pigeon got within his reach he took hold of it to eat it, when Van Inwegen caught the hawk and found him to be old and starved, and had become unable to procure his food.

Different opinions have existed in relation to the government of the actions of animals, birds and other creatures. In respect to which, it is difficult in many cases to determine whether certain of their actions are governed by the dictates of mind, to answer certain purposes, or by an impression on their natures to cause their actions without design. The cravings of food and other bodily desires emanate from the nature created in their bodies. The way and manner of each species to procure its food are dictates of the mind, in which some, if not all, display as much tact and correctness to obtain their objects as the mind of man could direct in their respective bodily capacities. The fear of an enemy, or of danger from any cause, is a dictate of the mind and affects the body, and both will unite their efforts to defend or escape the danger the means of which the mind directs, and the body performs accordingly thereto.

The fox, the ground-hog and some other creatures dig holes in the ground, sometimes under and between rocks, in which to hide and escape from being caught by an enemy, and for a safe place to rest and sleep. The squirrels will seek places in hollow trees for their safety. The bears, which were here in former times, when cold weather commenced in November or December retired from the open woods into those which were thickly timbered with hemlock, and there sought and made places under rocks and roots of trees in which to lay up all winter, and continued in their respective places without eating all winter and remained fat. Hunters from this neighborhood sometimes went there in former times, in February or March when warm weather commenced, and found them with their dogs, and killed them in their holes, in which some were confined by the frost of the ground and were fat.

The beaver performs the greatest work of the animal species, which comprehends a more extensive source of enjoyments than what any other creatures have achieved, all of which appears to be a preconcerted plan of their own to obtain the results of their labors, but still may be, as some have thought, an instinct of their natures to do it without design. A company of beavers will unite, select the best place to build a dam across a stream of water where they can overflow the greatest extent of ground by damming the stream, and the company will all engage in the work cutting down brush and saplings with their teeth and bringing the same to the place selected for a dam, and there place them in the stream so as to form a dam, for which they make use of mud, clay and ground, to intermix with the brush, so as to confine in the dam both brush, ground, &c., and also to make it tight. After this work is all completed, a male and female will unite and dig a hole in the side of a bank, which the water will not overflow in times of freshets, and commence to dig it under water and raise gradually until they get into dry ground above the surface level of the water in times of freshets, where they make a place in which to lay, repose and sleep in safety, where wolves, dogs and enemies of every kind cannot find them. The pond also becomes a safe place for them, in which they can have their sportive exercises and furnish them with food. There was in ancient times a beaver-dam in this town near the bridge across Basha's kill, on the land of Abraham Cuddeback, Esq., which dammed the water so as to overflow a large tract of bog meadow land above the bridge. There also was a beaver-dam across the Old Dam Brook, on the land of Abraham J. Cuddeback, Esq., which also overflowed a tract of swamp and bog meadow land. There undoubtedly have been others in ancient times in this town. These were the two best places in this part of the town for Beaver dams, and were on streams not subject to freeze much.

It appears evident that the genius and natural activity of some animals and birds is greater than that of others, and that all possess thought, memory, discernment, and many of the passions and affections like those of human beings ; and have a degree of speech in which, by articulate sounds, they can inform each other of danger from an enemy, of the finding of food, calling each other to come and partake of it, or forbidding it ; and no doubt a great part of the different species of animals and birds, especially the latter, have more of an extensive language, to communicate to and with each of their respective tribes, than what man can discover. When a man happens to come unawares near to a partridge with young ones, she will give immediate warning to her brood to run and hide, and if the man pursues them, or comes near to them, she will approach to him and flutter as though she was unable to get out of his way, to entice the man to follow her, but will keep at such a distance from him that he cannot catch her; and in this manner she will lead the man away from her young in pursuit of herself, until he leaves them and her fear ceases, when she will return to the brood, call them to her, and attend to them in her usual way. Other birds also have their ways and means of causing their young ones to run and hide for fear of an enemy, and to entice him away from the place where the young chickens are hid. All animals will save and defend their young offspring to the utmost of their power, in which they generally make use of the best means they possess.

FOURTH GENERATION.

The fourth and a part of the fifth generations, descendants from four of the first settlers in the Peenpack neighborhood, are now on the stage of action, and those who have remained in Deerpark now own nearly all the valuable land for agricultural purposes in it; and, like their grandfathers, have generally stuck to the soil for their living. Yet a part of these two generations are now in other pursuits of life, embracing a great part of all the occupations which are followed in this part of our country. The former generally became transactors of business between the years 1810 and 1830. These, and their cotemporaries in our country, are within reach of nearly all the acquisitions which have been mentioned, and can procure such portions thereof as their means and abilities will admit, and which furnishes them with a vast amount of enjoyment of which their ancestry were destitute, and also are a source of many evils which they escaped by not having the means of their production. Now, in consequence of those changes, it requires more circumspection now than in former times to travel life's journey, from the existence of many by-roads, the worst of which are sometimes most enticing ; and these have obscured our way through life, and created difficulties in selecting the best course for the enjoyment of our additional acquisitions, without burdening ourselves with the evils which emanate from an erroneous choice.

When men become enabled to have a great variety of food and drink it bcomes necessary to know which are of a healthy character and which are pernicious thereto, so as to enable them to make a choice for its preservation in cases where that becomes the object, in preference to risking future evil consequences. So also when men are enabled to have all the desirable enjoyments of ease and comfortable dwellings, it is necessary for them to know how to occupy these without injuring their health, and also to have a knowledge of whatever has a tendency to promote or impair it. Much information relative thereto can be acquired from the writings of those who have studied and practiced the art of healing and preserving health.

Doctor Fowler of the city of New York has for some

years published a monthly water cure journal, in which he has treated extensively of the effects of water in curing diseases and preserving health, by using it in a proper manner to answer its different purposes. He has also treated on the bad effects of some of the habits of the people of our country and the consequences thereof. He also from time to time published a variety of articles relative to the causes of diseases and means of avoiding the same, &c. Doctor Nichols and wife, Mary S. Gove Nichols, formerly of the city of New York and afterwards residents of Cincinnatti, also published a similar monthly journal for a few years. From such works much interesting matter for the benefit of mankind can be acquired, and more than people generally are willing to practice.

The physicians, by much study and practice, have become very skillful in overcoming and curing disease, and more dependence is now had on their services for prolonging life than on any other means for that purpose.

Important as the preservation of health is to mankind, few appear to be willing to use means for preserving it, some of which are irksome and others counteract the cravings of nature. These latter differ widely in persons, and consequently are easier overcome by some than others. Many men of strong constitutions, in healthy employments, have little need of being strictly temperate, or to use extraordinary means to preserve health.

The three first verses of the XXIII chapter of the Proverbs of Solomon are very applicable in respect to making choice of a great variety of food and drink such as Rulers of his time furnished.

Now as man is composed of both body and a comprehensive and intelligent mind, which latter is subject to pleasure and pain, happiness and misery, it is necessary to use our best means for the welfare of both ; and as a large field is opened by the acquisitions mentioned, for the enjoyment of the mind as well as of the body, and also a large field for speculative objects, many of which are of a pernicious character, it becomes necessary to select such as will promote happiness and to shun those which are attended with dangerous consequences, both in respect to suffering corporeal punishment and the torments of a guilty conscience.

The most perfect course of life creates the easiest journey, but a perfect guidance in all respects is beyond the comprehension of man, and would not be fully pursued even if understood. Our country is filled with preachers to expound the laws of God and dictate the walks of life, yet men err to such a degree from a perfect life as to make it necessary to have many codes of civil law, and a great number of civil officers versed therein to prevent imposition and sustain the rights of man.

A perfect life of the mass of men in all respects would create the greatest happiness. It has been prophesied that a time will arrive when men will become blessed with a happy state of existence, when wars will cease and peace prevail. In respect of which, if we take a view of what has transpired in the world, it appears that mankind have made a great advance since the commencement of our historical revelations from a rude and barbarous state towards that of civilization, and from the numerous, cruel and terrible warfares of ancient times to a greater prevalence of peace and much less cruelty in warfare. Yet the world of mankind stlll remains at a vast distance from such a happy state as might exist if all men were disposed to act for the welfare of all, and had discernment to use the best means for obtaining it. But we still remain fallible in both those respects, and if ever we are to have the enjoyment of such a happy state it must be yet far in advance, and it probably is best to progress slowly and become fitted by degrees for such a change.

RELIGIOUS WORSHIP.

I have understood that there were religious reading meetings in the Peenpack neighborhood before the Rev. Fryenmoet commenced his ministerial services.

When measures were first taken by the inhabitants along the Neversink and Delaware rivers, for a distance of about 45 or 50 miles down the same, to procure a preacher for the people throughout that distance, there was not a man in its vicinity qualified to preach the Gospel, and, in consequence of this district then being sparsely inhabited, the people united and formed four congregations, to procure the services of one preacher, and agreed with John Casparus Fryenmoet, a young man from Switzerland who had previously studied for the ministry, to furnish him with money to go to Amsterdam in Holland, finish his education and become ordained, after which he was to serve them as their preacher. The sum they gave him for that purpose was £125 12s. 6d., equal to $314.06. He went, obtained his education and became authorized to preach the gospel, returned and commenced to preach for the four congregations in June 1741 ; but no agreement had yet been made in relation to his salary and other matters which were necessary to be agreed on, and before any agreement was made Fryenmoet received a call from Rochester. It appears, however, that he declined that call, and an agreement was entered into between him and the church officers of Minisink and Mahackemeck congregations, the 7th of January, 1742, whereby it was stipulated that each of those congregations should pay Fryenmoet £20, equal to $50. A like sum paid by each of the other congregations made the amount of his salary $200 ; besides this he was to have 100 skipple of oats for horse feed, of which each congregation was to furnish 25 skipple. In February, 1745, the four congregations agreed to pay each £17 10s. for the purpose of building a house for Fryenmoet.

It appears from the church records that John Casparus Fryenmuth, born in Switzerland, with Eleanor Van Etten, born in Nytsfield, were married with a license from Governor Morris, in New Jersey, by Justice Abraham Van Camp, the 23d of July, 1742. The church records contain the rules and regulations of the church made at different times, which, in some respects, were different from those of the present time, among which were the two following, to wit : Church Wardens before officiating had to bind themselves in writing to remain subject to the Classis of Amsterdam. Persons intending to be married had to make out a certificate of their intended marriage and deliver it to the minister, who for three successive Sundays, at the close of service, read the certificate and at the same time gave notice that if any legal objections to the marriage existed, they should be made in due time and place.

This last continued to be practiced during Van Benschoten's services.

These records are in the Holland Dutch tongue. It appears that Fryenmoet's services ended in 1755 when his services became impracticable in consequence of the French war, whereby this frontier settlement became much exposed to Indian warfare, and he removed to Kinderhook, N. Y., where he preached for 21 years and where he died in 1778. He was represented as a man of short stature, handsome and eloquent.

One hundred and ten communicant members were received into the church whilst Fryenmoet officiated, within the congregations of Minisink and Mahackemeck, about 36 of whom resided in the present town of Deerpark. Of the latter the following from time to time alternately served as members of the Mahackemeck consistory :

Jacobus Swartwout, Anthony Van Etten,
Thomas Decker, Johannis Westbrook,
Johannis Decker, Solomon Koykendall,
Gerardus Van Inwegen, Josias Cole,
Peter Gumaer, Benjamin Depuy,
William Cole, Philip Swartwout,
Peter Kuykendall.

In the year 1760 the Rev. Thomas Romeyn commenced his ministerial services for the congregations mentioned, and continued until the year 1772, during which time a general attendance was given to his preaching, and reading meetings were had and attended also on those Sundays when there was no preaching in this congregation. This practice continued during the time of the successive ministers, until preaching was had every Sunday in our church. (Mr. Romeyn on leaving here settled in Canghnawaga, Montgomery County, N. Y., where after 21 years of ministerial labor he died in 1794.)

Within the time of Romeyn's services a schism occurred in the Dutch church, in consequence of the subordinate state of the church to the Classsis of Amsterdam, in Holland, in respect to ordaining ministers there, &c., which having become burdensome to many who had to go there to become authorized to preach the gospel, measures were taken to have a Classis established in this country for that purpose. This created two parties, one of which, termed Conferentie, was in favor of continuing according to former practice, and the other, termed Coetus, were advocates of a Classis formed in this country to examine and ordain men to preach the gospel. Of the former, Romeyn was a moderate adherent, probably in consequence of his ordination in Holland, yet the people of his congregations generally attended to his preaching and were not as violent partisans as many people were in some other parts of our country; and it is probable his services would have continued, if a few of the most influential ruling members of his church, who were of the Coetus party, had not projected means to end his services in the year mentioned.

From this time, a term of thirteen years elapsed in

which these congregations had no regular preacher, but probably had a few supplies before the Revolutionary War commenced, during its continuance, and after it ended.

In the year 1785 the Rev. Elias Van Benschoten entered on his ministerial services for the three congregations of Mahackemeck, Minisink and Walpack, in each of which he preached every third Sunday, in both the Dutch and English languages and generally performed half in each tongue; and required of the young people as their duty, to commit to memory in the English tongue the Heidelberg catechism, in such portions as he directed to be answered at each time of his preaching in the congregation, either on the same Sunday or on one of the days of the same week, at which time he gave explanations of that portion of the catechism. He retired in 1795, * and removed to a farm or tract of land he had purchased, situated east of the Shawangunk mountain, in the northerly part of New Jersey, on which he made great improvements and granted it to Mr. Cooper, a nephew of his by marriage, subject to payment by installments, and his money he bestowed for educating youths for the ministry, &c. ($17,000 given to the General Synod of Reformed Dutch Church for this purpose in 1814.)

Van Benschoten was a man well calculated for the rudeness of the time in which he officiated in those congregations.

After Van Benschoten's services were ended, a term

---

* Mr. V. B. moved to his farm in the Clove near Deckertown, N. J., in 1792, where he preached to the church organized under his ministry. He likewise preached occasionally to the churches in this valley until 1799. He died at the Clove in 1815.

of about four years elapsed before another regular preacher served this congregation. In, or about the winter of 1803 and 1804, the Rev. John Demarest commenced his services for the congregations mentioned and performed one-half of his preaching in the Dutch tongue, and the other half in English. He continued until about the year 1806. * After this a term of about ten or eleven years elapsed in which no regular preacher officiated in this congregation, but supplies were sometimes had.

On the 25th of January, 1817, the Rev. Cornelius C. Elting was installed pastor of the two congregations, Mahackemeck and Minisink, and performed his services in the English language. He died the 24th of October, 1843.†

All religious services have since been performed in the English tongue in our congregation. Within the term of his services a new church was built in Port Jervis, after which the name of "Mahackemeck Church" was altered by an act of the Legislature, in 1838, to that of "The Reformed Dutch Church of Deerpark." The materials of the old church were removed after the new one was finished, and the spot where the first and second churches had stood during a term of about one century, from the time the first was erected until the last was taken down, became vacant, and the ancient and latter occupants who formerly repaired to it for the worship of their Creator now generally sleep in their graves.

On the 29th of February, 1844, the Rev. George P.

---

* Mr. Demarest died in New York city in 1837.

† Mr. Elting is the only minister of this Church who has died during the pastorate of the Church.

HISTORY OF DEERPARK. 161

Van Wyck was ordained and installed pastor of the Reformed Dutch Church of Deerpark, unconnected with the congregation of Minisink, and his services were generally had every Sunday in this church, which he continued until in May, 1852.* On February 22d, 1853, the Rev. Hiram Slauson was installed pastor, and continued his services until in October 1857.†

In the year 1853 the church edifice at Cuddebackville was built at a cost of $2,500, principally borne by the inhabitants of that place and its vicinity. A church was organized March 12th, 1854, (by a committee of the Classis of Orange) consisting of thirteen members, twelve of whom were received from the Reformed Dutch Church of Deerpark, and one from the Episcopal Church of Middletown. The Rev. Henry Morris was installed as the first pastor of this church the third Tuesday of September, 1855. ‡

On the first Sabbath in February, 1858, the Rev. Samuel W. Mills commenced his pastoral services for the Dutch Reformed Church at Port Jervis.*

As we now generally have preaching every Sabbath, our reading meetings have been discontinued. The exercises of those meetings were prayer by one of the communicant members, and singing before and after reading a sermon from a book of sermons.

The greatest supporters of those meetings were Benjamin Depuy, Esq., within his time of action, and afterwards Joel Whitlock. In the early part of Depuy's

---

* Mr. Van Wyck is now (1889) living at Washington, D. C.
† Mr. Slauson is still (1889) living at Whitehall, N. Y.
‡ Mr. Morris remained pastor of this Church until 1861 when he removed to Port Jervis, and subsequently, in 1867, to Binghamton, N. Y., where he died, in 1881, at 78 years of age.
* Mr. Mills continued pastor until Nov. 1871.

life he, and sometimes Jacob R. Dewitt, performed the reading in Dutch, but in the latter part of his life and afterwards it was done in the English language and continued to be done in that tongue.

Since the construction of the Delaware and Hudson canal and the New York and Erie railroad this town has received an additional population, who have built up the large and flourishing village of Port Jervis. These are from different parts of our country and from different countries in Europe and are of different religious denominations.

The greatest proportion of these are of English origin, and some of them are the most opulent in it. This village, commenced about the year 1828, now contains six churches, all of which are generally occupied every Sunday for religious worship, to wit: A Dutch Reformed as mentioned, and a Baptist, Methodist, Presbyterian, Episcopalian and a Roman Catholic, (and now in 1890 a German Lutheran). The different opinions of men in religion and politics have always had a tendency to create enmity; but as men have become enlightened, those causes have gradually ceased to have such violent effects as in former times, especially in religion. The members of the different denominations in our town now harmonize in their business transactions, and their different opinions in religion do not effect their social intercourse in other respects. But in politics we must always expect to have times of great contention, if we continue to have the liberty of speaking our respective sentiments, for people will always disagree, both honestly and dishonestly in respect to certain matters which will, from time to time be introduced for legislative action and determination; and our inability to judge correctly in relation to all the numerous matters which will continually occur for such decision, together with many selfish views, will always cause strife in our political affairs, and these will continue to have a great effect in opening the eyes of the people in relation to our political matters.

In religion it is probable that the different denominations will generally continue to become freed from that enmity which formerly existed in consequence of their religious opinions, the folly of which is now apparent to the best informed part of mankind. The use of force and arms in former times to compel men to unite or keep united with certain religious sects, had a tendency to produce hypocrisy, for self preservation, but not to alter men's opinions. Convincing proofs are the only means to alter erroneous opinions, but the great evil of ancient times consisted in organizing men to answer selfish purposes by religious and political subjugation; the most numerous and powerful of each of these becoming united, created a power to tyranize over their opposers.

The acts of men which have emanated from the influence of serving God have been directed in many different ways, some of which have been very erroneous and contrary to the spirit of Christianity, although transacted by its professors. Such have been all the instigators of wars for selfish purposes, without a just cause, and all unjust impositions for whatever objects.

Within the present century much has been done to enlighten mankind and improve their condition, and we are under great obligations of gratitude to all the scientific men of our country for the vast improvement and discoveries they have made within my own time of life, most of which has been done by descendants of English origin, whose ancestors generally came into this country poor, to enjoy liberty in the wilds of the Eastern states, where they had to suffer the hardships of procuring a livelihood in a wilderness country, among the hazards of being exterminated by the numerous Indians who inhabited it. Now, notwithstanding their privations and all the hazards which attended their situations, they persevered, improved the country wherever they settled, defended themselvei against Indian hostilities, and, as soon as practicable, introduced religious worship, literature and the study of the arts, and sciences, and became the most enlightened people in our country.

Many of their descendants have emigrated into the different States of the Union, and, wherever they have located, they have generally introduced religion, literture, and the study of the arts and sciences. They occupy the greatest part of the most important stations of life in our country, and we are indebted to them for a vast amount of improvements, and for many manufacturing establishments in different parts of our country. In religion they do not all unite. Their spirit of liberty generally dictates the individuals to join such Christian denomination as they respectively prefer, in consequence of which they have become divided generally among the different Christian denominations in our country. These different opinions in religious sentiments generally create no enmity between the most enlightened professors, who so differ in opinion where no apprehensions of evil consequences exist, but indications of these have not become wholly extinguished, and may or may not prove an injury to the welfare of our country.

ADMINISTRATION OF JUSTICE.

For about 60 or 70 years the inhabitants of that part of the present town of Deerpark, which formerly was in the town of Mamakating in Ulster County, had no nearer Justice of the Peace than in Rochester, in the same County, which was about 35 or 40 miles distant from the Peenpack neighborhood ; and the services of that officer were unnecessary for the inhabitants of that neighborhood during that time, in which they had the honesty and prudence to adjust all matters relating to their mutual dealings. And the inhabitants of the lower neighborhood, who were in the County of Orange, and had settled there about 20 years after the settlement was made at Peenpack, must have resided there about 40 or 50 years before any Justice officiated in that neighborhood.

I presume that Jacobus (James) Van Auken was the first Justice of the Peace in the present town of Deerpark, and that he received his office from the authorities of the State of New Jersey before the line between the States became settled. He resided in the lower neighborhood. It was said that he was entirely illiterate, and that the wife of his son Daniel Van Auken, Leah Kittle, had been educated and could read and write, and did the same for her father-in-law when it became necessary for transacting his official business, in consequence of which she received the name of Justice in his time of life.

Benjamin Depuy and Philip Swartwout, Esquires, officiated as Justices of the Peace for the County of Ulster before the Revolutionary War commenced, and Anthony Van Etten and Solomon Kuykendall, Esquires, officiated as Justices of the Peace for the County of Orange, also before the commencement of the war, how long previous thereto I cannot determine, but think they must have come into office after the French war ended and before the year 1770. After the decease of Swartwout, Van Auken and Van Etten, which occurred, as has been mentioned, in the time of the war, Harmanus Van Inwegen became a Justice of the Peace of the County of Ulster and Levi Van Etten of Orange County. The former was a resident of the old town of Mamakating, and the latter of the former town of Minisink. Afterwards Peter G. Cuddeback became a Justice of the Peace of Ulster County, and officiated until he removed to Cayuga County.

After this time several individuals held the office in succession for the County of Orange, which became so altered, together with an alteration of the towns, as to include the present town of Deerpark in which Cuddeback resided. When the first and second churches of Mahackemeck congregation were built, a bench with a roof over it was made in each of those churches for a seat of such magistrates in time of divine service.* When those civil officers were first introduced into this part of our country they were more highly esteemed

---

* This was very common in the Dutch Churches in this country at that time.

than at present, though it did not require as good abilities and as much law knowledge to discharge their duties honorably in former times as at present, in consequence of the great increase of their business and a more general diffusion of law knowledge, also by having become familiarized among the people in a much greater degree than formerly.

The descendants of the first settlers in the two neighborhoods mentioned have generally settled all their mutual dealings without the process of law, which has so continued to the present time ; and before the Revolution the Justices must have had only a mere trifle of business. After the war ended law prosecutions and trials began, and their increase a few years thereafter made a great addition of business for the resident Justices in the towns mentioned, which rapidly augmented until the County of Sullivan was formed and became established out of a part of the old County of Ulster, and a part of the latter added to the old County of Orange, which transferred a great amount of law business from the present County of Ulster into the County of Sullivan.

After the Reuolutionary War, the large forests of wild lands then in Ulster County contained a great amount of valuable pine, oak and hemlock timber, both near the Delaware river and for some miles distant from it. This valuable property became an object of enterprise for people to get and convey to market, first generally in the form of logs. Few owners of the land were in this part of the country, which gave people the opportunity to get it where they saw fit, but as the business extended owners were found and many people became engaged in manufacturing the timber into boards, scantling,&c., and into hewed timber, staves and shingles for market. Among these quite a great proportion of the residents in the former and present towns of Deerpark engaged, in which some did a small business, others on a medium scale, and some to a very great extent. This, with few exceptions, was done on a credit system, by running in debt to merchants and farmers for the necessary supplies the individuals wanted for their business, which generally was made payable every ensuing spring and fall, at which time the lumber was run down the river to market. In progressing in this manner many disappointments occurred which caused failures in making payments according to agreements, in consequence of disasters on the river, unsteady prices of lumber and of the produce necessary for that business, wages, &c., and many other causes of failures contributed to make business for justices and constables of the old County of Ulster, who resided in the former town of Mamakating. As early as 1792 when I was constable and a resident of that town, I had to travel several times a distance of between 15 and 40 miles to serve processes for recovery of debts from persons who resided along the river between Pond Eddy and Cochecton, and who were in poor circumstances to pay debts. These lumbered under great disadvantages in getting round timber from the mountains bordering on the river, which business they had commenced after the war ended.

After the war terminated, boards and other sawed timber were much wanted for building purposes within the present town of Deerpark, where the enemy had burned the buildings of the inhabitants, and these materials were not manufactured in this vicinity at that time. It became necessary to build saw mills to furnish those articles, and three men, Capt. Abraham Cuddeback, Benjamin Cuddeback and Capt. Abraham Westfall, built a saw mill on a brook at that time termed Bush-kill, at or near the present tanning establishment of Mr. O. B. Wheeler, near the bridge across the Neversink river on the Mount Hope and Lumberland turnpike ; and three other men, Benjamin Depuy, Esq., Elias Gumaer and Samuel Depuy, built a saw mill on the present premises of Abraham Cuddeback, Esq., on the same brook on which his present saw mill stands.

Near the Bush-kill saw mill at that time was much pine timber, and that mill continued to do considerable business for several years, and the same, and a few other mills west of it, manufactured the greatest part of the boards formerly used for the buildings in Orange County, and the shingles for roofing the same were generally made in the vicinity of those mills. All of which, during a certain period of time, made a great business, and some addition to that of our Justice's courts originated from it.

A great trading intercourse generally creates many causes of contention and fills our courts with a great amount of business, all of which has its bad and good effects, and while some bear the burdens of contention others receive the benefit of transacting the necessary business for adjusting matters of dispute. All the consequences resulting from such an intercourse of mankind, have a tendency to enlighten them, and, according to the old saying " It's an ill wind that blows nobody any good."

ANTERIOR PRICES OF LIVE STOCK, GRAIN AND OTHER FARMERS' PRODUCE, WAGES, &C.

For many years the prices of those productions, wages, &c., were about stationary. At what time or times these were established is uncertain, but I presume it must have been as early as 1740, when the same became regulated according to the discretion of the people throughout this valley or by the Esopus merchant, and continued until about the year 1790. The farmers generally paid mechanics and laborers with the produce of their farms, and the latter paid what they bought of the former in labor, and very little money was in circulation among them.

CURRENCY AND MEASURES.

Previous to the Revolutionary War, and for a few years after it ended, the currency in circulation here was that of the Colony of New York, afterwards termed

State of New York, which was calculated in pounds, shillings, pence and farthings.

1 pound was 20 shillings................$2.50
1 shilling was 12 pence .... .12½
1 penny was 4 farthings................. .01 1-25

The grain measure was a skipple, and held 3 pecks. The cloth measure was an ell, ¾ of a yard long.

For brevity, the prices annexed to the following articles, wages, &c., is in our present currency, and the measures are those now in use.

LIVE STOCK.

Horses, from about................$20.00 to $50.00
Cows, " " .... 7.50 to 12.50
Sheep, " " .... 1.00 to 1.50

GRAIN.

Wheat, per bushel............................$0.75
Rye, per bushel............................. .50
Corn, per bushel............................ .50
Buckwheat, per bushel....................... .31

MEAT.

Beef, per cwt...............................$2.50
Pork, per cwt............................... 4.00

CLOTHS.

For man's every day wear linen, unbleached, per yard...$0.44
For man's every day wear linen, bleached, per yard... .50
Finer qualities for Sunday wear at higher prices, linsey-woolsey, fulled and colored........ 1.00

Unfulled plain colored linsey-woolsey for woman's
    wear .... .75
These cloths were all woven five-quarters of a yard wide.

FLAX.

Unhatcheled, per lb......................... $0.09
Tow, per lb................................. .06

WAGES.

For labor on a farm, per year, from... $50.00 to $75.00
For labor on a farm, per month, from.. 5.00 to   7.50
For labor on a farm, per day, except
    in harvest and haying, from.... .25 to .37½
Per day for cradling grain................... $0.62½
Per day for mowing grass.................... .50
Raking and binding after a cradler........... .62½
Raking only after a cradler.................. .25
Binding after a cradler...................... .37½
Cutting timber and splitting it into rails, per
    hundred .... .37½
Splitting rails, per hundred................. .18¾
Crackling or breaking flax per hundred handfulls. .12½
Swingling flax per lb. about................. .03
Spinning it for common wear per lb. (women's
    work) .... .12½
Weaving linen for every day wear per yard about. .04
Linsey-Woolsey per yard about............... .07

CARPENTER'S WORK.

Per day from...................... $0.50 to $0.72
For making the woodwork of a wagon........ $25.00
Of a lumber sleigh........................... 1.50

Of a plow............................... 1.00
Of a fanning mill....................... 12.50

MASON'S WORK.

Per day from................ ....$0.50 to $0.75

The sums paid for the mason and carpenter's work of the dwelling house of Peter Gumaer, done about the year 1753, will show how cheap those mechanics worked at that time.

The house was 45 by 40 feet on the ground, with a cellar under the same, divided into four cellar rooms and four dwelling rooms. The walls were of stone, masoned with clay mortar and were about two feet thick, pointed outside of the house and inside of the cellar rooms with lime and sand mortar, and plastered inside of the rooms and chamber with mortar of lime, &c. The mason work of this house was done by three masons, by the job, for £30, equal to $75; and the carpenter's work was also done by the job, by a Mr. Wells, for the like sum of £30, equal to $75.

To show how cheap these mechanics worked, I have thought proper to give a further description of this house, being as follows, to wit: The two side walls were about 20 feet high from the bottom of the cellar to the plates, and the two end walls were about 28 feet high. The two walls, which divided the cellar and dwelling house each into four apartments, were about 16 feet high from the bottom of the cellar to the chamber floor. The two chimneys, with the supporting walls in the cellar and forming the fire-places, were about 40 feet high from the bottom of the cellar to their tops, and were each about 10 x 6 feet square above the upper floor, from which they were tapering towards the top of the roof, and above it were about 4 or 5 feet square.

The carpenter's work consisted of hewing, fitting and laying the cellar beams, which were about one foot square, and reached from the outside to the inside walls, also hewing, planing and laying the beams of the upper floor, which were of pitch pine timber and about 14 x 10 inches square, also hewing and planing the plates on which the roof rested, also hewing the rafters, which were about 8 x 6 inches square at the lower ends and about 5 inches square at the top end and those on the sides were about 32 feet long, and those on the two other sides, or ends, were about 26 feet long, and each pair of the long rafters contained a girth of about 25 feet long and about 8 x 6 inches square. The lath on which the shingles were nailed were of split timber, hewed $1\frac{1}{4}$ inch thick and about 5 inches wide, the shingles were of white pine timber 3 feet long and 1 inch thick at the butt end, shaved to near an edge at the other end ; the lower and upper floors were of pitch pine boards, $1\frac{1}{2}$ inch thick planed on the side within the rooms.

The house contained 7 inside panel doors, four outside framed doors, and four cellar batten doors, five windows, which contained each 24 panes of glass, and panel window shutters to each window, four small windows above the outside doors and eight small chamber and cellar windows, and a large closet each side of one of the fire places. These two jobs were paid in money, which was of much more value at that time than at present.

Few country dwelling houses contain as great a weight of materials as were put into this building. It lasted until the year 1823, and, with a little repairing and a new roof, might have stood and been a good house until the present time. It contained all its first materials except a small repair of the floors before each fire place, and rebuilding the east wall, from which the pointing had been washed by northeast storms of rain and caused it to fall. The lower and upper floors, and the two end roofs, were yet water tight when the house was taken down. The roofs on the north and south sides had become leaky, and more on the north than south side. The two end roofs were very steep, and those on the sides were somewhat steeper than roofs of the present time.

BUSINESS TRANSACTIONS OF OUR ANCESTORS.

As there has been a great change in the business transactions of people in this part of the country generally within the last half century, I have thought proper to give a more particular statement in relation to that of the inhabitants formerly of our present town, than what has been mentioned in the preceding part of this work.

Commencing with the ending and beginning of the year, I will in the first instance narrate the manner in which Christmas and New Year's days were kept.

CHRISTMAS AND NEW YEAR'S.

The day preceding Christmas, preparations were made to enjoy some good diets on that and the next succeeding day, by baking cakes, boiling doughnuts, &c., on which to feast, especially the second Christmas day, when neighbors visited each other and partook of the good victuals previously and this day provided. Formerly two days were kept as Christmas, and two days as New Year's throughout our valley. The first Christmas day was kept holy and reverential as Sunday, and the second as mentioned, on the evening of which the young people generally had a dance. The day previous to New Year's, the same preparations were made for both New Year's days, and early in the morning of the first day, at or before break of day, a few individuals would be out in one part of the neighborhood and salute a near neighbor with the firing of guns by his door, which awakening the inmates they speedily arose out of their beds, and, on meeting their visitors, they mutually greeted each other with the wish of a Happy New Year, after which a treat of cider was given and sometimes other liquor after it became used, and some cakes, doughnuts and apples were distributed among them. Here they were joined by one or a few of this family and proceeded to the next neighbor, where the same routine was gone through and generally one or a few individuals were added at each house, and by this means quite a company was formed by passing through the neighborhood. In my time these proceedings began to be disapproved, and gradually ceased until they became abandoned. In all other respects, the first and second New Year's days were kept in the same manner as the second Christmas day.

After these festivities were past, the people resumed their business, which was very urgent at this time of the year, in which, before my time, it was said there generally was good sleighing and they had to do a great amount of teaming in the winter season while sleighing continued, to get their wheat to market, their fire wood, post and rail timber drawn, and much other work which teams had to perform. Wheat, in the first instance, had to be taken between 50 and 60 miles distance from our present town to market, afterwards between 40 and 50 miles.

As the days are short in winter, the people before my time occupied a part of the night after dark in the evening and in the morning before daylight, for threshing and cleaning wheat, and also for taking it to market. The great amount of fire wood, post and rail timber, which had to be provided in the winter season, also made much winter work. After sleighing ended, post and rail timber had to be split, the posts holed and rails sharpened, and, as soon as the frost was out of the ground, new fences were made of these and the old fences were repaired. In 1770 and afterwards, a great amount of fuel and fencing timber was used in consequence of the large fires farmers kept up in their sitting rooms and kitchens, the smallness and scattered situation to which farms had become reduced at that time, and the necessity of dividing them into small lots for pasturing purposes.

In March and April, the flax which had not been previously dressed, was in these months all crackled and swingled, rope yarn spun, and ropes made for halters, traces, lines and other uses. Each farmer in these months prepared his hides for tanning, procured white oak bark, and laid down the hides, together with the bark and water, in troughs, to be tanned during the warm season. The linen for summer wear was principally woven in these months by the men, the manure drawn from the barnyards and stables, and flax seed and oats sowed.

In May, the corn-ground was ploughed and planted, and ploughing for buckwheat was done for the first time.

In June, the corn was hoed twice, for which it was prepared by plowing each time between the rows one way, so that much had to be done with the hoe, and the ploughing for summer fallow was also commenced, and at an early day of the settlement sometimes finished in this month.

In July the harvesting and gathering of winter grain and oats, and the pulling of flax was all done.

In August, after meadows were made, the grass was cut and gathered for fodder, flax taken up and brought into barns, and a second ploughing for wheat was principally done in this month. (It was customary with the ancient people to plough three times for wheat and twice for rye).

In September the plowing for seed and sowing winter grain was commenced, and was continued during the month of October and beginning of November. Cider was from time to time made during these three months. The topping of corn, by cutting off the stalks above the ears for fodder, was done in September until the time of the Revolutionary War, after which this practice was abandoned and the cutting up of corn near the ground and setting it up in small shocks became a general practice, in which, improvements in performing the work, and time and manner of doing the same, have from time to time been made. Until the time of the Revolutionary War, and during that war, the ears of corn on the stalks, standing out in the field after becoming dry, were pulled from the stalks and thrown into small heaps between the rows, from which they were taken with a wagon into the barn where they were husked, sometimes by means of one or more husking frolics, but more generally by the family only. In these months and beginning of December, flax was rotted, and some of it dressed for winter spinning, and rope yarn was spun, and ropes made for cow-ropes, halters, traces, lines and other purposes for winter use.

In November, winter apples, and the few potatoes, turnips and other roots raised in those times, were brought into the cellar ; and the killing and putting up of pork and beef was done in the latter part of this month and beginning of December. The manufacturing of leather, which each farmer had tanned during the season, was done at this time and made into shoes, (generally by a member of the family), also the weaving of linsey-woolsey and woolen check for winter wear, and the dressing of some flax for winter spinning. In November, each farmer generally took a load of wheat and flax seed to market, for procuring salt, pepper, iron and other articles.

The women, as well as the men, had also to perform a great amount of labor. Besides their ordinary housework, they had to spin the yarn for all their clothing, hatched their flax, and card their wool, bleach all their linen for shirts and some other uses, make all the wearing apparel of both men and women, and did all the knitting of stockings and mittens, which amounted to more than double the knitting now done for a family, which had become necessary in consequence of the fashion of men in former times wearing short breeches, which also made it necessary for them to wear over stockings.

All those necessary occupations made a great amount of business for our ancestors, and furnished them with a very plentiful supply of the necessaries of life. They had very little help besides that of a few slaves, which generally did not amount to more than a man and a woman slave to a family, exclusive of children and old people not able to do much. The inhabitants were generally farmers, and few laborers could be obtained by them.

CHARACTERISTICS.

The characteristics of each individual by a marriage union becoming changed in their children, form characters differing, in some degree, from those of each parent, which, being continued from generation to generation, gradually extinguish those of the original parents; but to what extent of time or how many generations would have to succeed each other before these would all become extinguished the writer cannot determine. By bringing into calculation the first pioneers as the first generation, the sixth, and a part of the fifth and seventh, are now, in 1861, on the stage of action. In many individuals of the fifth and sixth generations are yet remains of the characteristics of their respective, most anterior parentage. These are more prominent in some of the descendants than in others, and also have been inherited in a greater degree in some families than in others, and certain predominating characteristics of an anterior ancestor have been the most prevalent in the line of their descent.

CHARACTERS OF SOME OF THE FIRST SETTLERS.

Very little is now known respecting the seven first pioneers. I imagine that they had all been in comfortable circumstances of life, and had become reduced so that they were in want of means for a livelihood, and became associated to obtain possession of some good land which they were not able to purchase in the settled part of the country, and had to venture to emigrate into its wilds which remained unsettled by white people but was inhabited by Indians, who at that time were thought to be a more savage and cruel people than what they in reality were.

The three Swartwouts, we have reason to presume, were best calculated for this enterprise, and that their companions must have had much reliance on them for protection. Not only were they possessed of superior capacities in respect of body and spirit for adventurous undertakings, but also were a very social, jocose, humorous and witty people, well calculated to become easily familiarized with strangers and court friendship, which first qualities were necessary to intimidate the Indians, and the latter to court and maintain friendship with them. They were an easy people and made no great exertions to acquire property by means of hard labor, but provided for a good living. Some of these characteristics have become much changed in the descendants of those who remained in this vicinity, and some of them have been inherited to the present time. The Swartwout character became much changed by the union of Major Swartwout with the daughter of the first Peter Gumaer, whose only surviving son, Philip Swartwout, became the greatest business man of his time in this neighborhood. He also was more sedate and economical than his ancestors; in other respects he had inherited the Swartwout character. A great degree of these existed in the two succeeding generations, and have not become extinguished in the sixth.

Caudebec and Guimar, reduced from a state of affluence to that of indigence, differed widely to meet such a change and undertake the task of manual labor for a living which became necessary after they landed in this country, and was undertaken by them, but, as they were not able to perform as much as men habituated to it, they received only low wages. Caudebec, being dissatisfied, told Guimar that he would not work for such low wages; Guimar replied that they had to do something for a living, and, as they could not do much, they could not expect much, and that while they labored they had their living, if no more. At the instigation of Caudebec, they went from the State in which they first landed into the State of New York, and he, having been habituated to a trading business, became introduced into the family of Benjamin Provost, who also were in such business, and was married to one of his daughters. Guimar, in the meantime, undertook the business of cleaning flax by the pound, for which he received wages according to what he did, and also became married to a daughter (as has been supposed) of a Deyo.

After these two individuals became settled in our present town, the same difference continued to exist in relation to their business transactions. Guimar, with the help of his daughters, two slaves he bought or had of his father-in-law, and one son, (his youngest child), became the greatest farmer in this town. He was very persevering in his business transactions, and severe to compel his slaves, also his daughters and son, to do all the labor they could perform. The daughters, five in number, although of delicate constitutions, did all the housework and manufacturing of all their clothing, also a part of the work on the farm and taking wheat to market. He, himself, dressed all his flax, to which business he had become habituated before he settled on his farm, which was about all the farmer's work he could do. He also was severe to enforce the moral and religious duties of his children. His descendants have, from generation to generation, very generally inherited his persevering business character to the present time; in other respects many of his characteristics have become extinguished.

Caudebec was the reverse of Guimar in respect to his business transactions, and more tender towards his children. He had much of a speculative disposition, and aimed at getting a living by easier means than that of steady manual labor, and this probably was the view of the seven first settlers and cause of their emigration to get possession of land where wild animals, fowls and fishes abounded, which, together with the cultivation of small portions of such land, would furnish means for an easy life and a better living, in respect of eatables, than what we can now enjoy.

After those individuals became located in our present town, it was necessary for them to procure a title for the land they wanted to occupy, and it appears that they selected Caudebec, as the most proper person, to send to the Governor and procure a patent for as many acres of land as would cover what they wanted to occupy.

After one of the Swartwouts, Caudebec and Guimar became owners of the patent right, they had to contend for the possession of a great part of the land they claimed and had in their possession, and it was necessary for them to devise means to counteract those who wanted to dispossess them. Caudebec, who was of a contemplative mind, must have been well calculated to assist in forming plans for that purpose, and I have understood that he, and certain individuals of his own family, officiated in some of those which were very important.

After his daughters became married, he devised means for their livelihood, by inducing the husbands of three of them, Abraham Louw, Evert Hornbeck and Harmanus Van Gordon, to locate on the east side of the Delaware river, in the State of New Jersey, opposite Shipikunk Island ; and also his son James and two of his brothers-in-law to do the same, and each of them take possession of as much land on the island as was necessary for a livelihood for his respective family. This island was a body of very good river land, and the first possessor of any part of it had a right to hold what he had in possession without paying for it. It was termed King's land, and to remain unsold by his Majesty or Government. Other islands in that river were in the same situation, and the husband of another of his daughters, Westfall, located himself on the same side of the river, opposite Minisink Island, and took possession of a part of that island.

From all of which we must infer that he was a man well calculated to overcome difficulties, and had a penetrating mind. He was characterized as a sensible man. He had been educated, but to what extent is not known. He had told his family that he had been a great reader before he left his country, and that he regretted that his children did not have the opportunity to become educated. He instructed them in moral and religious duties, and was very tenacious of their characters. At a certain time two of his daughters told him that certain persons had made a scandalous report respecting them. He asked if it was true what they had said. They replied no, it was all lies. "Well," said he, " maintain good characters and let them talk; they will get ashamed of their lies."

His character, in relation to what has been mentioned respecting his mental ability, has been inherited from generation to generation by some of his descendants (who remained in this town) to the present time. The bodily capacities of his sons, in respect of size, strength and agility, I consider to have been inherited from his wife, which, although much reduced from that of those ancients, is still superior in some of the descendants of the present time to that of the generality of men. Some of those ancients, in our neighborhood, were a very talkative people and uncommonly fond of conversation, in which they embraced a great variety of topics in relation to what had transpired in this valley for a distance of sixty or seventy miles, and included a great many remarks in relation to the conduct of the people of those times and much argumentation on different subjects. I have sat many a long winter evening, and many an hour in the daytime, to hear the conversations and arguments of a few of the individuals of the second generation. These propensities, which were inherent in this family, have become much changed in their descendants of the present time. Many of these communications, remarks and arguments were entertaining and instructive, and had a tendency to induce good morality, of which they possessed more in principle than in language. I will here introduce one good remark, which one of them made in the presence of myself and a few others, which was that, " The first of anything from which trouble accrued was the cause of all the evil consequences which originated from the same."

In bodily size, strength and agility, there was a great similarity between the Swartwouts and Cuddebacks, but those I have known differed in visage. It was said that some of the ancients were superior in personal beauty and natural mental abilities to their descendants. This information I have had from different sources. The first time I saw Nathaniel Owen, who kept a store and tavern many years ago, about two miles east of the Wallkill, on the road to New Windsor and Newburgh, he told me that he had been acquainted with the old people in our two neighborhoods, and that he had never been in a place where there was so great a proportion of portly, handsome men as were in those neighborhoods, which he considered as remarkable for such a by-place as this was at that time. He named Major Swartwout, the second Peter Gumaer, William Cuddeback, Johannis (John) Westbrook and the first Peter Kuykendall as the most superior in those respects, and that their children generally were inferior to them, not only in bodily capacity, but also in natural mental ability. The ancient Swartwouts, Cuddebacks and Gumaers had black, curly hair and generally blue eyes and fair skin. The first Van Inwegen had red hair, his son Gerardus had black, curly hair and his children had black hair.

Harmanus Van Inwegen's character has been represented in this work as a bold and fearless man, which is about all that is now known respecting him. This was well known by Anthony Swartwout, Jacob Cuddeback and the first Peter Gumaer, before they procured him to locate in their little neighborhood for their assistance in defending the premises they claimed. His co-operation with them was important for all these four individuals, for he, as well as the others had become interested therein by having a portion of the land granted to him by the others, and as the saying is " He became a great spoke in the wheel" to maintain their possessions. He was always honored by his companions for his bravery and help in their struggles. He and they continued to live near neighbors in friendship and harmony until death ended their lives.

Van Inwegen had only one son (Gerardus) and one daughter (Jane). Gerardus lived a very near neighbor to my father, and I was familiarly acquainted with him in his old age for several years previous to his death. I did also sometimes see his sister; they were both small and very lean in flesh during the time I knew them, and their skin was much wrinkled, (which latter denoted they had been more fleshy in earlier life) they appeared to be more healthy and were smart for their ages. Gerardus retained his health until old age ended his life, and after his death it was said of him that he died a natural death, of old age, without sickness.

The characteristics of the father and son of this family have not been generally inherited by the children and grand-children. It has been said that Cornelius Van Inwegen, Jr., father of Moses Van Inwegen, resembled and took more after his great-grandfather, Harmanus Van Inwegen, than any other individual of all his descendants. Moses, his son, has some resemblance to his father, but I consider him to take more after the ancient DeWitt family than that of any other. There were certain traits of character which some of the children and grand-children of Gerardus inherited from him, but generally they took more after other families from whom they were also descendants.

Many of the ancient characteristics of both the Swartwouts and Cuddebacks still remain in their descendants, but I consider James D. Swartwout as possessing those of the ancient Swartwout family in a superior degree ; Col. Peter Cuddeback as having the greatest resemblance to the ancient Cuddeback family; Abraham Cuddeback, son of Col. William A. Cuddeback, when in prime of life, appeared to have more of the character of his grandfather, Capt. Cuddeback, than any other of the descendants of the latter; James Devens, Esq., grandson of the second Peter Gumaer, had some resemblance of his grandfather. But all these differed in some respects from the originals.

Benjamin Hornbeck, a grandson of Capt. Cuddeback, had much of the penetrating mind of his grandfather.

EMIGRATION FROM THIS TOWN.

Enumeration of families who were in this town during the time of the Revolutionary War, and of those who removed out of it after the war ended, and of those who now, in 1861, remain in it of those descendants of those ancients, including marriage connections.

First of those of the upper or Peenpack neighborhood, two of whom, DeWitt and Terwilliger, were no descendants of the first four families.

The names of the heads of those families were the following, to wit :

Capt. Jacob R. DeWitt, Capt. Abraham Cuddeback,
Benjamin Depuy, Esq., Benjamin Cuddeback,
Abraham Cuddeback, Jacob D. Gumaer,
Elias Gumaer, Harmanus Van Inwegen, Esq.,
Cornelius Van Inwegen, Philip Swartwout, Esq.,
John Wallace, Peter Gumaer,
Matthew Terwilliger, Ezekiel Gumaer,
Capt. Abraham Westfall.

Of these, their children, grand-children, and great-grand-children who had formed marriage connections, and together with these had become families, the following number have, from time to time, removed from this neighborhood, to wit :

Name.	No. of family.		
	Of parents' children.	Of grand-children.	Of great-grand-children.
Jacob R. De Witt	8	4	0
Benjamin Depuy	7	2	0
Abraham Cuddeback	3	1	0
Elias Gumaer	7	0	0
Cornelius Van Inwegen	6	3	2
John Wallace	3	0	0
Matthew Terwilliger	4	0	0
Capt. Cuddeback	4	8	5
Benjamin Cuddeback	4	14	0
Jacob D. Gumaer	6	1	2
Harmanus Van Inwegen	3	15	0
Philip Swartwout	3	3	0
Peter Gumaer	3	1	0
Ezekial Gumaer	0	1	0
Abraham Westfall	1	0	0
	62	53	9

62+53+9= 124.

This emigration amounts to 124 families and now, in 1861, there remain 30 within the former limits of the neighborhood; gives the amount of 154 families of descendants of the men named and have formed families by connected marriages. These had their living during the time they remained in this place from the productions of the small patent of 1200 acres of land, and although it had become reduced to a low state of cultivation, more of its productions have been transferred to other people than would have supported another such a number of families. Emigration commenced about the year 1790 and has continued to the present time. The families first mentioned of, DeWitt, Depuy, Cuddeback, Gumaer, Van Inwegen and Wallace, settled on the military lands in the state of New York at Onondaga and at the Owasco and Skaneateles Lakes at an early period of the settlement of those lands, and some were among the first pioneers of the same where they all procured lands and became farmers in very comfortable circumstances, and many of their descendants, like their forefathers, have also sold their farms and removed into the western states to advance their interest for the benefit of their children. The other families have removed in all directions from this neighborhood at greater and less distances from it, but generally into the western part of this state and into Pennsylvania and different other states.

Of the four first families, who remained permanent residents in this neighborhood, twelve children became married to non-residents of the same and founded twelve families, two of which settled in the lower neighborhood and were among the first settlers in it, five in the State of New Jersey, four in Rochester and its vicinity in Ulster County, and one in Orange County, east of Shawangunk mountain. The other children of those ancients were seven in number, and formed only six families. These remained in the neighborhood until about the year 1790. From this it appears that only half as many families of the first descendants remained in it as what moved out of it, or settled in other places.

Now, if the 12 families mentioned had become settled and remained in the neighborhood, together with the other six, and increased and emigrated, in the same proportion of the latter, the amount, after deducting those of DeWitt and Terwilliger numbering 16, would now be 324 emigrated, and 90 of present residents, and the whole amount 411 families.

INCREASE OF POPULATION.

As no accurate calculation can be made of the whole number of families descended from the first four permanent residents in this neighborhood, I have adopted a rule for obtaining the number of those now in existence as near as the same can probably be arrived at without actual enumeration, by getting a ratio of increase of the first, second, and as much of the third, generation as I can ascertain ; also the whole number of these from the time of the commencement of the first to the present time, in manner following, to wit :

The first four families had an increase of 18, and these had an increase of 66 families, and 27 of the latter had an increase of 129. This enumeration is made from a knowledge I have in relation to those ancients. Of these, however, there were two families of the second generation whom I could not determine, but have estimated them at the same average rate of increase as that of the others, and the remaining 39 are estimated to have produced an equal proportion of population, according to their number, as that of the 27, which latter giving an amount of 129, the remaining 39 will give an amount of 186, and both these amount to 315 families of the third generation. The average increase of each of these per family is as follows:

First   4 give a ratio of......................4½
Second 18   "   "   " 3¾
Third   66   "   "   " 4¾

These being compounded give an average ratio of about 4½ families to one. Now a greater proportion of the fourth and fifth generations have died younger than of the three first, in consequence of which I have reduced the increase of the two former to that of a ratio of three per family, being about one-third lower than those enumerated. This is a great change for the term in which the alteration has occurred; still, the latter is about the same rate of increase as that of the United States since the year 1790 to the present time. In respect of foreign access of population the proportion which the former has acquired by intermarriages cannot differ much from that which the latter has acquired by immigration from Europe and by the importation of Africans to enslave them.

The year 1700 I contemplate to be about the medium point of time between the births of the oldest and the youngest children of the first four families, from which to the present time is 161 years and reaches on an average about the beginning of the sixth generation and leaves two unascertained whose increase on a ratio of 3 is as follows, to wit: $315 \times 3 = 945 \times 3 = 2835$ families of the present fifth generation; and exclusive of these there must now be a great proportion of the fourth generation in existence, and that the whole of the present families of descendants mentioned cannot be less than 3200 now on the stage of action. The greatest part of these are now widely dispersed into different parts of our country.

The five generations have had their growth within a term of 161 years, which gives an average of 32 years for each.

LOWER NEIGHBORHOOD.

Enumeration of families in the time of the Revolutionary War, embracing the head of each family, to wit :

—————— Decker.
Jacob Schoonover,
Moses Cortright,
Abraham Van Auken,
Johannis Westbrook,
Johannis Decker,
Major John Decker,
Sylvester Cortright,
Anthony Van Etten, Esq.,
Levi Van Etten,
Jacobus Van Fliet,
Daniel Van Auken,
Solomon Kuykendall,
Simeon Westfall,
Wilhelmus Cole,
Peter Cuykendall,
Martinus Decker,
Samuel Caskey,
Jacobus Davis,

Of these families, their children and grand-children, the following number of families have removed out of this town:

NAMES.	No. of parents and children.	No. of grand-children.
———— Decker	2	
Jacob Schoonover	1	
Moses Cortright	1	
Abraham Van Auken	3	
John Westbrook	2	
John Decker	3	
Maj. John Decker	3	6
Sylvester Cortright	2	
Anthony Van Etten, Esq.	6	3
Levi Van Etten	1	4
James Van Fliet	1	4
Daniel Van Auken	11	5
Solomon Kuykendall's heir or devisee, James Van Fliet, Jr.	3	
Simon Westfall	4	
Wilhelmus Cole		3
Peter Kuykendall	4	4
Martin Decker	2	
Samuel Caskey	1	
James Davis	6	1
	56	30

There may have been a few other families who have removed out of the town whom I have not known.

Of the descendants of those ancients, there now remain, as near as I can ascertain, about 5 families in this neighborhood.

These numbers, 56+30+5=91 families.

There now are about 20 families in this neighborhood who are of the anterior emigration from the upper neighborhood and are included in in its calculations.

The following is a calculation of the number of families of each generation of the lower neighborhood, to wit:

1st generation which was contemporary with the
   second of this upper neighborhood........ 20
2d.. 91
3rd, at an increase of three families to one.......273
4th, at the same rate of increase.................819

The two last 273+819=1,092 families. To this last number add the 3,000 of the upper neighborhood and the amount is 4,092.

There are two of these prior generations who, by deaths, may fall short of these numbers mentioned, but I contemplate that as great an addition of families exists of the succeeding generation of each neighborhood as will amount to such loss, and that there now are at least 4,000 families in existence of descendants in some degree of the ancients mentioned.

THOMAS WHITE.

This man's services have been of greater benefit and advantage to the third generation of descendants of our neighborhood than those of any other individual, in consequence of which he ought to be held in remembrance by our descendants, and he, together with ourselves, become incorporated in our history as the first important originator of education in it. In justice to the merits of Mr. White in respect of myself, I will here state that by means of his services I have become enabled to write this history and exhibit to its readers the information it contains; and in addition thereto the enjoyment of other sources of knowledge for which and all other blessings we have reason to be thankful, not only to the individual from whom we derived the same but also to that Being who is the originator of all our enjoyments.

The benefits we (who were of the generation mentioned) have derived from him, consisted in the literature he taught us in our childhood and youth at short different periods of time in the schools he kept in our neighborhood, whereby we generally received such a portion of education as enabled each of us to transact his own ordinary business in relation to his dealings with others, which, in our time, had become more necessary than what it was in the days of our forefathers, most of whom kept no written memoranda of their dealings with each other, which in their time (during about ninety years) was unnecessary for the greatest part of them. In addition to these benefits we became more enlightened and enabled to acquire additional knowledge and information by reading, &c. Mr. White and his wife Elizabeth, came to this neighborhood in the autumn of 1776 (as near as I can ascertain) to serve its inhabitants as a schoolmaster and they became residents in my father's house together with his own family, and taught school in one of its rooms during the ensuing winter, and probably until some of the neighbors moved into it and the construction of a fort commenced, and notwithstanding the danger to which the inhabitants of our town became exposed by the invasion of the Indians, he continued to live in the house during a great part of the war, and was in it at the time when the fort was attacked.

When the enemy came in sight, he told Capt. Cuddeback that he was a King's man, but would stand by him to help defend the fort against those savages to the utmost of his power. (He was a warm friend of his native country and its laws). Mr. White was in the fort during the hard winter in the time of the war, and kept a diary from which he ascertained that no water had dropped from the roof of the house during a term of forty days in that winter.

I will here, before proceeding further with the history of Mr. White, narrate how the inmates of the fort managed to sustain themselves during the winter. When the Indians burnt the houses of the neighbors, many of the pots were damaged by these fires. These were used for keeping small fires in them in different parts of the fort house. Two large fires were generally kept up in the two front rooms, and a fire in a stove in another, and in the other room a pot with hot coals, supplied from the fire places, was kept up to warm the room for a dwelling of some of the oldest women. On the chamber, against the sides of the chimneys, pots with fire were kept, supplied with hot coals from the fire places, and also with chips and small pieces of wood.

In the northwest corner of the chamber, a small room was partitioned off for a dwelling of Mr. White and his wife, so that in winter time they were out of the great bustle of those who were in the house. A pot with fire in it was also kept in his room, and sometimes a small fire was kept in one of the foremost cellar rooms for a few soldiers. After the snow became too deep to get wood from where it was previously got, the men first broke a road to a large hickory tree, which stood in a field, under cultivation, of Benjamin Cuddeback, at about one-quarter of a mile distant from the fort. This was cut up and brought to it. The butt log, about three feet thick in diameter, was cut through and served for a log in each fire place. The next log contained all the knots of its large limbs, and could not be cut through nor split with powder, and remained there until it became rotten, long after the war ended. Next a road was broke through the snow about the same distance of the first road, to the Neversink river, which (in ordinary winters generally remained open from the mouth of Bashas-kill to the Delaware river, about ten miles distant) was all frozen over with strong ice, so that teams could pass on it.

Along the east bank of the river, trees were cut, so as to fall on the ice, and thereby the men were enabled to get a plentiful supply of wool. In passing to and from the river, a spring brook had to be crossed, which in other winters generally remains open at the place where it was crossed that winter on strong ice. Much snow blew into the brook and coalesced with the water, and all froze together and formed thick, strong ice, so that teams passed over it during the coldest weather in that winter.

I will here resume my history in relation to Mr. White. A few years before he came into the neighborhood, a school house had been built in its central part, about twenty-five rods southwest of Capt. Cuddeback's residence. Mr. Thomas Kyte had been employed to teach school in this house, but, in consequence of much other business, the school was much neglected and very little education was acquired by those he taught, and after he quit, the neighborhood luckily obtained a good teacher by employing Mr. White. He had emigrated into this country from England where he had received his education, and also acquired the trade of manufacturing ropes. He said that every youth in England (when he was there) had to learn a trade, even the King's son, who was expected to become heir to the Crown, had to learn a trade, and that the King, who reigned when he was there, had been taught the trade of weaving silk.

Mr. White was a small, light-built man, very active and quick to perform the business he transacted. The action of his mind was also quick, and more suitable for acquiring a great amount of superficial knowledge than to penetrate and make deep researches into sciences which are difficult to be understood, for which a bright mind of slow action is more suitable. He was also a man of uncommon perseverance to transact the business of his trade, the teaching of his schools, &c., and, whenever he was not employed in either of these, he was generally engaged in reading or writing which he would pursue to a very late hour in the night ; and early in the morning, at or before break of day, would be up out of bed, assist his wife to get breakfast, and resume his business. He was very fond of association and delighted to give and receive information, which induced him to write a great many letters to his distant friends and acquaintances, in which he was very expert and never at a loss for matter to make out a long letter, whenever he felt inclined to do it.

I conclude that Mr. White had been taught in one of the best of common schools in England, and in a very perfect manner as far as he had progressed. He was a very eloquent reader, and could perform the same with an air suitable to the nature of the subject on which the reading treated. I have always considered him to have been equal to the best of readers I have ever heard. He was also very perfect in orthography ; arithmetic he did not understand as well as some other teachers we have had since his time. He said he had passed through the greatest part of Dillworth's arithmetic at school, but had forgotten some of the rules in the latter part of his assistant, which contained more arithmetic matter than the books now generally used in our common schools. He had some knowledge of the Greek and Latin languages, and as much of the French tongue as enabled him to interpret the French words which were interspersed in different parts of a book I read in school the last year he taught in our neighborhood, and, by much reading, he had acquired an extensive knowledge of the English tongue. He said that when at home in his country (which he always called his home) he had free access to a library of books, and that he had read many of them on different subjects, whereby he had received the greatest part of his historical and other information of different kinds.

After his last year's service in our neighborhood he retired to the east side of Shawangunk mountain, into a neighborhood of his former residence, where he continued a few years. During this time, and one or two years previous to it, Moses DeWitt, a son of Capt. Jacob Rutsen DeWitt, a resident of this neighborhood who had, in his youth, become the best scholar in Mr. White's school, and afterwards received a small addition thereto, became well qualified for a surveyor, and was employed as an under-surveyor, when he was about twenty-one years of age, to run the line between the States of New York and Pennsylvania, and afterwards to survey some Government lands at, and in the vicinity of, Tioga Point, and thereafter he and Maj. Hardenbergh obtained the whole business of surveying the military lands in this State. While DeWitt was occupied in that business he concluded to locate in the County of Tioga, and induced Mr. White to move into it. The latter, after becoming a resident in it, became its County Clerk. Mr. DeWitt's mind became changed in respect to locating himself, and he settled in the County of Onondaga. After Mr. White's term of service as County Clerk ended, he removed to the residence of Mr. DeWitt, whose health had become impaired by exposure in the pursuit of his business of surveying, and his constitution continued to debilitate until he was taken with a severe sickness, which, after a short duration, ended his days at the age of about twenty-seven years, at which time he had acquired an estate, in wild lands, worth about ten thousand pounds, New York currency. During the time he was confined to his bed, Mr. White was his affectionate and faithful attendant, but his services did not avail to prolong life, and all hopes of enjoying the remainder of his life, together with his friend, were ended.

After a short stay he removed from the place, which had become a melancholy situation to him, into the

County of Orange and bought a small farm in the westerly part of the town of Wallkill, in the neighborhood where his former friends and acquaintances, Elijah and Elisha Reeve, Esqs., Erastus Mapes, Hezekiah Woodward, Alsop Vail and others, lived, where he not only became so situated as to enjoy the happiness of associating with them, but also had access, whenever desirable, to his friends and acquaintances in his former neighborhood on the west side of Shawangunk mountain. Mr. White had no children nor any relatives in this country to attract his affections; these, consequently, became more strongly directed towards those individuals who were the most agreeable to him. He remained in the neighborhood of his residence until death ended his mortal life, and, after his decease, was buried in the graveyard at the Presbyterian church near Otisville. In and by his last will he made several small bequests to his friends, as memorials of his friendship towards them. He also directed the sum of six hundred and twenty dollars, of the avails of his estate, to be kept at interest, payable annually, for the purpose of paying for preaching one sermon in each one of four different Congregations, annually, forever, one of which was the Dutch Reformed Congregation now in Deerpark, (formerly Mahackemeck Congregation), which appears in and by the will to have been intended for the inhabitants of Peenpack, to whom he had become much attached during the different periods of time he resided in it, and consequently also for the benefit of their descendants.* He also bequeathed a few other small legacies

---

* The other three Churches were the Congregational Church at Middletown, and the Episcopal and Presbyterian Churches in Goshen.

to his best friends in the neighborhood of his last residence.

The characteristics of Mr. White exhibited indications of his having been descended from a respectable family in his native country. He possessed very honorable and honest principles, also those of morality and piety, which were apparent in his transactions and walks of life, and also in the doctrines he generally advanced when those qualifications became a subject of discourse.

THE END.

CONTENTS.

	Page.
Preface.	7
Introduction.	9
Statement by Committee on Publication with sketch of the Author. *	13
Geographical Formation of Valley	19
Game, Fowls, Fish, Fruit, &c	22
Indians	24
Manufacture of Implements of Iron and Steel	27
First Settlers—Who they were and whence they came	30
Ancient Families of Peenpack	41
Ancient Families of Lower Neighborhood	68
Longevity of First and Second Generations	78
Lower Neighborhood	85
Population of Peenpack, Manner of Living, &c., during Revolutionary War and later	86
Forts in Peenpack and Occupants	86
Forts in Lower Neighborhood, with some of the Occurrences during the War	89
Habits and Manner of Living	96
Use of Cider and Spirits	101
Use of Spirits at Funerals and Weddings	102
Treating Visitors	104
No Drunkards among Them for One Hundred Years	107
Physical Strength of First Generation	110

---

* The statement by the Committee on Publication which appears on pages 13-17 should have preceded both the Preface and Introduction. By an oversight not discovered until too late for correction it became displaced and appears out of its proper order.

Page.

Some Prominent Characters — Major James Swartwout, William Cuddeback, Peter Gumaer, Gerardus Van Inwegen, Samuel Swartwout, Capt. Abraham Cuddeback, Benjamin Depuy, Philip Swartwout, Anthony Van Etten, Cornelius Van Inwegen. 114
Minisink Battle........................ 127
Great Changes in Agriculture, Manufacture, Travel and Improvements of Every Kind.. 137
Scarcity of Physicians in Former Times....... 144
Birds, Reptiles and Animals................ 145
Health, Food, &c........................... 152
Religious Worship—Organization of Reformed Dutch Church and its Ministers.......... 155
Administration of Justice—First Justice of Peace 165
Prices of Stock, Grain, &c., formerly.......... 170
Currency and Measures..................... 170
Wages 172
Cost of Building a House.................... 173
Business Transactions and Employments of Ancestors............................. 175
Christmas and New Year's—Two days devoted to each................................ 175
Characteristics of some of First Settlers and their descendants...................... 180–1
Emigration from Town of Deerpark........... 189
Increase of Population..................... 192
Thomas White............................. 196

-A-

ADAMS
  Mary (Cuddeback), 46
  Samuel, 46
AVILLAGUER
  L., 54
  S., 54

-B-

BENNET, 144
  Dr., 144
  James, 72
BRANDT, 90
BRINK
  Betsy (Rosecrantz), 48
  Blandina (Westfall), 73
  Fennetje, 73
  John, 73
  Manual, 48
  Reuben, 73
BROOKS
  Mr., 122
BULL
  Catherine (Rosecrantz) (Decker), 48
  Crissie, 48
BURNET
  Rachel (De Witt), 66
  Robert, 66

-C-

CARPENTER
  Benjamin, 72
CASKEY
  Cornelius, 58
  Samuel, 89, 91, 194, 195
CAUDEBEC, 33, 34, 35, 182, 183, 184
CHAMBERS
  William, 31
CILLFAND
  Losary, 54
CLINTON, 65
  Dewitt, 65
CODEBACK, 33
COLE, 43
  Catrina, 62
  Cornelius, 74
  David, 60, 76
  Josias, 74, 157
  Leah (--), 85
  Leah (Westbrook), 74
  Lena (Rosecrantz), 48
  Margaret, 60, 82
  Maria, 74
  Maria (Cuddeback) (Westfall), 43
  Martyne, 48
  Sarah, 72, 73, 85
  Tjaetje, 53
  Wilhelmus, 74, 85, 89, 91, 194, 195
  William, 73, 157
COLLUM, 31
COOPER

COOPER (continued)
  Mr., 159
CORTRIGHT
  --- (Van Etten), 69
  Daniel, 69
  Henry, 69
  Margaret (Decker), 69
  Moses, 69, 89, 90,
    194, 195
  Sylvester, 89, 195
CORTWRIGHT
  Sylvester, 90, 194
CUDDEBACK, 31, 32, 33,
    34, 37, 39, 40, 67,
    79, 81, 84, 85, 105,
    108, 117, 121, 122,
    128, 129, 186, 187,
    188, 191
  Capt., 8, 78, 83, 92,
    93, 121, 127, 131,
    134, 188, 189, 190,
    198, 199
  Widow, 92
  --- (Provost), 37
  Ab., 92
  Abraham, 41, 42, 44,
    46, 48, 52, 58, 59,
    70, 79, 87, 88, 92,
    111, 119, 147, 150,
    169, 188, 189, 190
  Annatje, 46
  B., 92
  Benj., 93
  Benjamin, 41, 44, 45,
    53, 70, 79, 87, 92,
    110, 126, 169, 189,
    190, 199
  Captain, 41
  Catherine (Van Fliet),
    45, 53
  Cornelius, 44
  Dinah, 42, 46, 79
  Eleanor, 42, 43, 46,
    47, 79
  Else, 43, 79
  Elsie, 49
  Elting, 70
  Esther, 44, 46, 48
  Esther (Gumaer), 44,
    58
  Esther (Swartwout),
    41, 46, 52, 79
  George, 58, 60, 89
  Harmanus, 47
  Henry, 45, 58, 60, 89
  Isaac, 70
  Jacob, 24, 30, 31, 39,
    40, 41, 44, 48, 63,
    64, 78, 79, 110, 121,
    187
  James, 41, 44, 45, 46,
    79, 111
  Jane (De Witt), 46, 67
  Jemima, 44, 45
  Jemima (Elting), 41,
    44
  Jemmia, 133
  John, 46
  Joseph, 43, 48, 69
  Levi, 45, 92
  Margaret (De Witt),
    46, 67
  Margaret (Provost),
    41, 44
  Maria, 43, 79
  Mary, 46

CUDDEBACK (continued)
  Naomi, 43, 56, 79
  Neelje (Decker), 41
  Neyltje (Decker), 45
  Neyltje (Westbrook), 45
  Peter, 44, 46, 60, 166, 188
  Philip, 46, 92
  Richard, 46
  Roolif, 79
  Roulif, 45
  Samuel, 45
  Sarah, 45, 53, 79
  Seynta (Van Fliet), 46
  Syntche, 45
  Thomas, 70
  William, 41, 44, 45, 53, 64, 79, 111, 115, 187, 188
CUDEBACK, 46
CUYKENDALL
  Peter, 194

-D-

DAVIS
  Anna, 68
  Beletje, 76
  Catharina, 76
  Daniel, 68, 76
  Deborah (Schoonover), 76
  Elizabeth, 68, 76
  Elizabeth (Kater), 68, 76, 83
  George, 76
  J., 92, 94
  Jacobus, 76, 194
  James, 68, 76, 83, 89, 195
  Joel, 76
  Jonas, 76
  Lea, 76
  Leah, 68, 83
  Leah (Decker), 76
  Mary, 73
  Petrus, 76
  Polly, 68
  Salomon, 76
  Samuel, 73, 76
  Solomon, 68, 76
DE WIT
  Taitie, 55
DE WITT, 188, 189, 191, 192, 202
  Capt., 83, 92
  Mr., 202
  Charity, 55, 56, 57
  Egbert, 65, 66
  Elizabeth, 53
  Esther, 66, 67
  Hannah, 66, 67
  J.R., 46, 94
  Jacob, 46, 53, 59, 65, 66, 83, 88, 162, 189, 190
  Jacob Rutsen, 202
  Jane, 46, 59, 60, 66, 67
  Jane (Depuy), 65, 83
  Margaret, 46, 66, 67
  Mary, 66
  Moses, 65, 66, 202
  Rachel, 66
DECKER, 53, 91, 194, 195

DECKER (continued)
  Major, 89, 91
  Benjamin, 62
  Catherine
    (Rosecrantz), 48
  Catrina (Cole), 62
  Christopher, 41
  Daniel, 48, 61, 62
  Deborah (Van Fliet),
    53, 85
  Eleanor (Quick), 74
  Elizabeth (De Witt),
    53
  Famitje, 74
  Hannah, 62, 85, 132
  Hannah (Van Inwegen),
    59, 61
  Henry, 70
  Hulda, 58, 63, 82
  Isaac, 53, 74
  Isaiah, 53
  Jacob, 74
  James, 74
  Jane, 62
  Johannis, 85, 157, 194
  John, 53, 58, 62, 75,
    76, 85, 89, 90, 91,
    194, 195(2)
  Joseph, 74
  Leah, 76
  Levi, 53
  Lydia, 74
  Margaret, 62, 69, 74
  Margaret (Gumaer), 58,
    62
  Margery, 53
  Martin, 76, 85, 89,
    91, 195
  Martinus, 85, 89, 91,
    194
  Mary, 62, 74
  Neelje, 41
  Neyltje, 45
  Peter, 62, 74, 89
  Richard, 76
  Sarah, 62
  Sarah (Hornbeck), 58,
    62, 85
  Seletta, 53
  Solomon, 74
  Thomas, 58, 59, 61,
    62, 69, 74, 132, 157
DEMAREST
  John, 160
DEPUY, 51, 84, 118, 130,
    131, 132, 191
  Esq., 8, 83, 86, 89,
    92, 94, 136
  Abraham, 47
  Benjamin, 47, 51, 59,
    67, 80, 88, 129, 157,
    161, 166, 169, 189,
    190
  Eleanor, 51
  Elizabeth (Swartwout),
    51, 80
  Esther, 51
  Esther (De Witt), 67
  James, 51, 67
  Jane, 65, 83
  John, 51
  M., 92
  Margaret, 51, 59, 82
  Martin, 47
  Moses, 47, 51, 65, 88
  S., 92, 94

DEPUY (continued)
  Samuel, 51, 88, 169
  Sarah (Louw), 47
DEVENS
  Abraham, 59
  Charity, 59
  Elias, 59
  Jacob, 59
  James, 59, 82, 188
  Mary (Gumaer), 59, 82
  Peter, 59
DEYO, 37, 183
DIMMICK, 73
DONALDSON
  William, 45
DUBOIS, 56
  --- (Guimar), 56
DURLAND, 52
  --- (Swartwout), 52

-E-

EAGER, 11, 20, 31, 45,
  65, 67, 90, 119
  Samuel W., 14
ELTING, 41
  Widow, 72
  Cornelius, 160
  Jan, 56
  Jemima, 41, 44
  Mary (Guimar), 56
  Peter, 56
ENNES
  Alexander, 49
  Daniel, 49, 67, 71
  Eleanor (Hornbeck), 49
  Hannah (De Witt), 67
  James, 49, 67

Margaret, 47
William, 47, 49
ENNIS
  Alexander (Saunder),
    48
  Roana (Rosecrantz), 48

-F-

FOWLER
  Dr., 152
  Samuel, 73
FREDENBURGH
  --- (Shimer), 71
  --- (Van Gordon), 50
  Aaron, 50
  Benjamin, 50
  Daniel, 50
  Hezekiah, 50, 71
  Joshua, 50
  Wilhelmus, 50
  Wilhemus, 42
FRYENMOET, 157
  Rev., 155
  J.C., 53
  John Casparus, 155
FRYENMUTH
  Eleanor (Van Etten),
    156
  Johan Casp., 133
  John Casper, 156
  Magdelena (Van Etten),
    133

-G-

GEEGGE
  Leah (Davis), 68, 83

GEEGGE (continued)
  W., 92
  William, 68, 83
  Wm., 94
GODEFFROY
  A.J., 30
GOMAR, 36
GOVE
  Mary, 153
GUIMAR, 36, 182, 183, 184
  Anne, 56
  Charity (De Witt), 56
  Esther, 55
  Esther (--), 53
  Mary, 56
  Peter, 53, 54, 56
  Pierre, 54
GUMAER, 10, 16, 32, 34,
    36, 37, 38, 84, 85,
    86, 93, 105, 106,
    108, 113, 117, 119,
    187, 191
  "Fort", 30
  Mr., 13, 14, 17
  A.E., 30
  Abraham, 59
  Andrew, 17
  Anna, 51, 55
  Anne, 50, 80
  Benjamin, 59
  Charity, 58, 59
  Charity (De Witt), 55,
    57
  Eb., 92, 94
  Elias, 37, 57, 58, 59,
    82, 88, 169, 189, 190
  Elizabeth, 55, 57, 58,
    59
  Esther, 44, 50, 51,
    55, 57, 58, 81
  Esther (--), 54
  Esther Harriet, 17
  Ez., 92, 94
  Ezekiel, 15, 17, 45,
    47, 54, 57, 58, 82,
    84, 87, 92, 189, 190
  Gerardus, 58
  Hannah, 58
  Hannah (Van Inwegen),
    58, 61
  Hulda (Decker), 58,
    63, 82
  J.D., 92, 93
  Jacob, 17, 57, 58, 63,
    82, 87, 125, 189, 190
  Jane, 58
  Maregretj, 57
  Margaret, 57, 58, 62,
    81
  Margaret (Depuy), 59,
    82
  Maria, 55, 57
  Mary, 55, 58, 59, 82
  Morgan, 17
  Naomi, 17
  Naomi (Louw), 47, 58,
    82
  Naomi (Low), 15
  P., 92
  Peter, 14, 15, 17, 30,
    36, 37, 39, 40, 41,
    44, 50, 54, 55, 57,
    58, 59, 61, 78, 80,
    81, 82, 87, 93, 94,
    111, 116, 144, 157,
    173, 182, 187, 188,

GUMAER (continued)
   189, 190
   Rachel, 55
   Ragel, 55
   Samuel, 59
GUMAR
   Peter, 55
GUYMARD, 36
   F., 54

-H-

HARDENBERGH
   Major, 202
HORNBECK
   --- (Cuddeback), 184
   --- (Guimar), 56
   Abraham, 48
   Benjamin, 43, 48, 62, 189
   Cornelius, 48
   Eleanor, 48, 49
   Eleanor (Cuddeback), 42, 47
   Elizabeth Ennes, 48
   Esther (Cuddeback), 44, 48
   Evart, 42, 44, 47, 48
   Evert, 184
   Henry, 44, 56
   Isaac, 56
   Jacob, 43, 48, 56
   Jacobus, 48
   James, 47
   Jane, 80
   Jemima, 48
   Joseph, 48
   Lena, 48
   Lodewyke, 56
   Lodiwyke, 43
   Lydia, 48, 49
   Lydia (Westbrook), 48
   Margaret, 48
   Margaret (Ennes), 47
   Maria, 44, 48
   Naomi (Cuddeback), 43, 56
   Philip, 56
   Rebecca (Wells), 48
   Saffrine, 48
   Sara, 48
   Sarah, 58, 62, 85
   Severyne, 48

-J-

JAMISON, 30, 39
   David, 30, 31, 40

-K-

KATER
   Elizabeth, 76
   Elizibeth, 68, 83
KETTLE
   Catharina, 75
   Leah, 71
KITTLE
   Leah, 165
KOYKENDALL
   Solomon, 157
KUYKENDAL
   Peter, 85
KUYKENDALL, 75
   Catharina (Kettle), 75
   Christyntje, 75

KUYKENDALL (continued)
  Elias, 74, 75
  Elizabeth, 75
  Famitje (Decker), 74
  Jacob, 73, 75
  Lea, 75
  Martin, 75
  Martinas, 75
  Peter, 74, 75, 91,
    157, 187, 195
  Sarah (Cole), 72, 85
  Solomon, 72, 75, 85,
    89, 91, 166, 194, 195
  Tjaetje, 73
  Wilhelmus, 75
KYTE
  Thomas, 54, 200

-L-

LAUX
  Ludwig, 89
LIVINGSTON
  Chancellor, 139
LOUW, 47
  --- (Cuddeback), 184
  Abraham, 42, 46, 58,
    184
  Dinah, 47
  Dinah (Cuddeback), 42,
    46
  Jacobus, 47
  Jane, 46
  Margaret, 47
  Naomi, 47, 58, 82
  Sarah, 47
  Tys, 42
LOW
  Naomi, 15

-M-

MAPES
  Erastus, 203
MASKRIG
  Daniel, 31
MATHER
  Mr., 122
MCGREGORIE
  Patrick, 31
MILLS
  Mr., 161
  Samuel, 161
MORIN
  Mr., 54
MORRIS, 34
  Governor, 156
  Mr., 161
  Henry, 33, 54, 161
  Huldah, 54
MULLOCK
  Esther Harriet
    (Gumaer), 17
MULOCK
  Isaac, 17

-N-

NEWTON
  Isaac, 16
NICHOLS
  Dr., 153
  Mary S. (Gove), 153

-O-

OWEN
  Nathaniel, 140, 186

-P-

PALMATIER
  Margaret, 52
PIERCE
  Johnathan, 88
PROVOST, 37
  Benjamin, 37, 182
  Margaret, 41, 44

-Q-

QUICK, 74
  Diana (Rosecrantz), 48
  Eleanor, 74
  John, 48

-R-

REEVE
  Elijah, 203
  Elisha, 203
ROMEYN
  Mr., 158
  Thomas, 157
ROSE
  Mary (De Witt), 66
  William, 66, 136
ROSECRANTZ
  Betsy, 48
  Catharine, 48
  Diana, 48
  James, 48
  Lena, 48
  Maria (Hornbeck), 48
  Roanna, 48
RUTTENBER, 31

-S-

SCHOONHOVER, 89
SCHOONOVER
  Deborah, 52, 76
  Jacob, 90, 194, 195
  Margaret, 85
SHELLEY
  Eleanor (Cuddeback), 46
  Samuel, 46
SHIMER
  --- (Ennes), 71
  Jacob, 70, 71
  Richard, 71
SLAUSON
  Mr., 161
  Hiram, 161
SLAVES
  "Woman", 83
  Anthony, 84
  Cuffee, 83
  Dinah, 83
  Frances, 83
  Jack, 84, 106, 126
  Jude, 84
  Peter, 83
  Susanna, 83, 84
SPRAGUE
  Mr., 124
ST.JOHN
  Stephen, 76, 89
STANTON
  Jonathan, 47
  Moses, 47

STANTON (continued)
  Sarah (Louw) (Depuy), 47
  William, 47
STOLL, 49
SUTHERLAND
  William, 31
SWARTWOUT, 37, 38, 39, 40, 59, 81, 84, 93(7), 108, 116, 132, 166, 181, 182, 184, 186, 187, 188
  Col., 52
  Esq., 81, 92, 131, 133
  Major, 81, 125, 182, 187
  --- (Gumaer), 182
  Anna, 52, 125
  Anna (Gumaer), 51
  Anna (Westbrook), 80
  Anne (Guimar), 56
  Anne (Gumaer), 50, 80
  Anthony, 30, 31, 39, 40, 50, 55, 80, 111, 187
  Antje (Wynkoop), 51
  Benjamin, 32
  Bernardus, 30, 39, 40
  Cornelius, 52, 144
  David, 23, 69, 74
  Deborah (--), 80
  Deborah (Schoonover), 52
  Elizabeth, 51, 80
  Esther, 41, 46, 52, 79
  Esther (Gumaer), 50, 51
  Gerardus, 38, 51, 52
  Henry, 67
  Jacobus, 38, 50, 51, 56, 157
  James, 39, 41, 50, 51, 52, 56, 71, 80, 84, 89, 93, 111, 114, 132, 188
  Jane, 51, 52
  Jane (Hornbeck), 80
  Major, 115
  Peter, 23, 32, 50, 52, 74, 80
  Philip, 51, 52, 80, 86, 131, 136, 157, 166, 182, 189, 190
  Samuel, 39, 50, 51, 55, 56, 80, 111, 117, 118
  Thomas, 30, 39, 40
SWEEZY
  Dr., 144

-T-

TERWILLIGER, 189, 192
  M., 92
  Matthew, 87, 93, 189, 190
TILLSON
  Jesse, 65
TOSHUCK
  David, 31
TUSTEN
  Col., 128
TYLER
  Capt., 127
TYSE, 30, 39
  Jan, 40

TYSE (continued)
    John, 30
TYSON, 30

-V-

VAIL
    Alsop, 203
VAN AUKEN, 70, 71, 85,
    166
    Miss, 71
    Abraham, 69, 70, 89,
        90, 194, 195
    Absolum, 71
    Cornelius, 69
    Daniel, 71, 85, 89,
        90, 165, 194, 195
    Elijah, 71
    Evart, 42, 49
    Evert, 48
    Grietje, 49
    Isaac, 48
    Jacobus, 165
    James, 42, 48, 49, 71,
        165
    Jeremiah, 71
    Joseph, 49
    Joshua, 71
    Josias, 69
    Leah, 85
    Leah (Kettle), 71
    Leah (Kittle), 165
    Margaret (Hornbeck),
        48
    Nathan, 71
    Nathaniel, 71
    Seletie, 49
    Seletta, 49

VAN BENSCHOTEN, 157, 159
    Elias, 159
VAN CAMP
    Abraham, 156
VAN ETTEN, 69, 132, 133,
    166
    Esq., 92
    Alida, 63, 133
    Anthony, 45, 62, 67,
        69, 85, 89, 90, 132,
        133, 157, 166, 194,
        195
    Antie, 133
    Antie (Westbrook), 133
    Antje, 62
    Blandina, 63, 67, 133
    Eleanor, 156
    Grannetje (Westbrook),
        133
    Hannah (Decker), 62,
        85, 132
    Hendricus, 133
    Henry, 62, 132
    Jacob, 46, 63, 133
    Jane (Louw), 46
    Jane (Westbrook), 49
    Janneke, 133
    Jemima (Cuddeback), 45
    Jemmia (Cuddeback),
        133
    Jenneke, 63
    John, 46, 68
    Levi, 49, 62, 76, 77,
        133, 166, 194, 195
    Magdelena, 133
    Margrieta, 63, 133
    Maria, 63, 133
    Solomon, 36, 58

VAN ETTEN (continued)
T., 76
Thomas, 62, 76, 77, 133
Tomas, 63
VAN FLEET
Solomon, 45, 51
VAN FLIET
--- (Carpenter), 72
--- (Swartwout), 80
--- (Westbrook), 72
Catherine, 45, 53
Clara, 53
Daniel, 45, 53, 72
Deborah, 53, 85
Elizabeth, 53
Esyntje, 53
Jacobus, 52, 194
Jacomyntje, 45
James, 52, 72, 85, 89, 91, 195
Jane (Swartwout), 51, 52
John, 45, 46, 51, 52, 53, 80
Mardochai, 45
Margaret (Palmatier), 52
Margaret (Schoonover), 85
Marie, 53
Marya, 53
Michael, 51, 53
Samuel, 53
Sarah, 45
Sarah (Cuddeback), 45, 53
Seynta, 46

Solomon, 45, 51, 53, 72
Thomas, 45, 53
Tjaetje (Cole), 53
Willem, 45
VAN GORDON
--- (Cuddeback), 184
Abraham, 50
Benjamin, 43, 50
Daniel, 43, 49
Eleanor, 50
Else, 50
Else (Cuddeback), 43
Elsie (Cuddeback), 49
Hannah (Westbrook), 49
Harmanus, 43, 49, 184
Lena, 50
Levi, 49
Martin, 50
Mary, 50
VAN INWEGEN, 39, 40, 84, 85, 105, 108, 134(2), 148, 187, 191
Esq., 84, 92, 93
--- (Swartwout), 38, 39, 59
Abraham, 61
Charlotte, 60
Cornelius, 31, 59, 60, 61, 82, 112, 126, 133, 188, 189, 190
Daniel, 61
David, 60
Eleanor (Westbrook), 60, 82
Eli, 73
Elizabeth, 58, 61
Gerardus, 38, 58, 59,

VAN INWEGEN (continued)
  60, 61, 82, 93, 111,
  116, 117, 147, 157,
  187, 188
  Hannah, 58, 59, 60,
    61, 82, 83
  Harmanus, 38, 59, 60,
    82, 87, 111, 166,
    187, 188, 189, 190
  Henry, 61
  Jacob, 58, 60, 61, 82
  Jane, 187
  Jane (De Witt), 59, 60
  Jenneke, 61
  John, 61
  Josias, 60
  Levi, 61
  Margaret, 61, 83
  Margaret (Cole), 60,
    82
  Martin, 61
  Mary, 61
  Moses, 188
  Peter, 58
  Samuel, 60
  Tjaade, 61
VAN NOY
  Joseph, 42
  Peter, 42(2)
VAN WYCK
  Mr., 161
  George, 160, 161

-W-

WALLACE, 191
  Cornelius, 61
  J., 92
  Jane, 61
  John, 61, 83, 87, 128,
    189, 190
  Margaret (Van
    Inwegen), 61, 83
WASHINGTON
  General, 131
WELLS, 48
  Mr., 173
  Rebecca, 48
WESTBROOK, 45, 47, 49
  Capt., 89
  Mr., 121
  Abraham, 47
  Alida, 70
  Anna, 80
  Anthonie, 70
  Antie, 133
  Antje, 70
  Blandina, 49
  Blandina (Westbrook),
    49
  Catherine, 49
  Cornelius, 49, 74
  Eleanor, 60, 82
  Elizabeth, 70
  Gideon, 70
  Grannetje, 133
  Hannah, 49
  Jacob, 48, 72
  Jane, 49, 72
  Jannetye, 44
  Joel, 70
  Johannes, 70, 194
  Johannis, 86, 157, 187
  John, 49, 70, 86, 90,
    121, 187, 195
  Leah, 74

WESTBROOK (continued)
  Lydia, 48
  Lydia (Hornbeck), 49
  Magdelena, 70, 86
  Margaret (Louw), 47
  Maria, 49
  Martin, 47
  Mary, 47
  Nancy, 47
  Neyltje, 45
  Saffrein, 49
  Samuel, 70
  Sara, 70
  Severyn, 49
  Solomon, 49
  Terrick, 60
  Tjeick, 49
  Utley, 89, 91
WESTFALL, 67, 76, 85, 185
  Abraham, 67, 169, 189, 190
  Aeltje, 72
  Annatje, 68
  Blandina, 72, 73
  Blandina (Van Etten), 67
  Daniel, 72
  David, 44, 73
  George, 43, 73
  Jane, 73
  Jane (Westbrook), 72
  Jemima (Cuddeback), 44
  John, 72, 73
  Joseph, 68
  Jury, 72
  Maria (Cuddeback), 43
  Mary (Davis), 73
  Reuben, 72, 73
  Sally, 85
  Samuel, 73
  Sarah (Cole), 73
  Simeon, 72, 73
  Simon, 45, 53, 72, 73, 85, 89, 91, 194, 195
  Solomon, 72
  Syntche (Cuddeback), 45
  Tjaetje (Kuykendall), 73
  Wilhelmus, 72
WHEELER
  O.B., 169
WHITE
  Mr., 197, 198, 199, 200, 201, 202, 203, 204
  Elizabeth, 197
  Thomas, 87, 126, 196, 203
WHITLOCK
  Aaron, 69
  Joel, 161
WILLIAMS
  John, 120
WILSON
  --- (Cuddeback), 46
  James, 46
WOODWARD
  Hezekiah, 203
WYNKOOP, 51
  Antje, 51
  Cornelius, 140

www.ingramcontent.com/pod-product-compliance
Lightning Source LLC
Chambersburg PA
CBHW050144170426
43197CB00011B/1958